完全掌握出題範圍 & 方向

強效衝刺！國中會考
搶分英單
2000

張翔 / 著

從 C 飆升到 A⁺⁺，

強到沒對手的**制霸祕笈**！

100% 針對會考量身打造，

培養零死角單字力，

單字 + 例句練習，

背誦更容易，輕鬆奪高分！

使用說明

100%破解國中會考單字之作！

熟記單字、掌握用法，英文 A++ 不再難。

高手絕招 1 會考必備 2000 單，一次囊括

拋開沉重的記憶負荷吧！針對會考高頻率 2000 單字編寫，讓你不再抱著單字書死記硬背，懂得掌握考點，分數就能輕鬆飆升。

Unit 01 Aa 字頭單字 ○ a/an ~ away ---- 008
Unit 02 Bb 字頭單字 ○ baby ~ by ---- 022
Unit 03 Cc 字頭單字 ○ cabbage ~ cute ---- 039
Unit 04 Dd 字頭單字 ○ daily ~ duty ---- 061
Unit 05 Ee 字頭單字 ○ each ~ eye ---- 075
Unit 06 Ff 字頭單字 ○ face ~ future ---- 085
Unit 07 Gg 字頭單字 ○ gain ~ gym ---- 099
Unit 08 Hh 字頭單字 ○ habit ~ husband ---- 107
Unit 09 Ii 字頭單字 ○ I ~ item ---- 118
Unit 10 Jj 字頭單字 ○ jacket ~ just ---- 124
Unit 11 Kk 字頭單字 ○ kangaroo ~ koala ---- 127
Unit 12 Ll 字頭單字 ○ lack ~ lunch ---- 130
Unit 13 Mm 字頭單字 ○ ma'am ~ myself ---- 139

006

高手絕招 2 隨掃Q Code，單字/例句全收

單字列表看累了嗎？換方式學，邊聽邊朗讀，比強自己盯著字母表好多了。給不同的學習刺激，成效更彰

高手絕招 3 單字完全解析，考點不遺漏

搶高分，比的不是記憶力，能精準抓到考試重點的人，才能脫穎而出。本書囊括必考字義 & 詞性，扎實地鞏固單字根基，會考十拿九穩。此外，以 A ～ Z 的順序編排，複習、查找更容易。

高手絕招 4

實用例句，在情境中強化記憶 & 應用

單字要記得長久，就從搭配例句下手！每個單字配例句，用情境加深記憶，同時順手習得單字的慣用搭配，提升語感。

稱霸會考

above
[ə`bʌv]
介 在…上面；超過

The summer camp does not accept teenagers above sixteen.
那個夏令營不接受超過十六歲的青少年。

abroad
[ə`brɔd]
副 在國外

補充 dormitory 宿舍
Amanda lived in the university dormitory when she studied abroad.
亞曼達在海外留學時，住在大學宿舍裡。

across
[ə`krɔs]
介 副 橫越；穿過

Chris took 17 days to drive across the United States.
克里斯花了十七天，開車橫越美國。

act
[ækt]
動 扮演 名 行動；法案

補充 opera 歌劇 / common 普遍的
In Taiwanese opera, it is very common for women to act male roles.
在歌仔戲中，女性扮演男性角色是很常見的。

action
[`ækʃən]
名 動作；行為

補充 romantic 浪漫的 / comedy 喜劇
Jenny loves romantic comedies more than action movies.
比起動作片，珍妮更喜歡浪漫愛情喜劇。

actor
[`æktə]
名（男）演員

補充 award 獎、獎品
The actor works hard at winning Golden Horse Awards.
這名演員努力地想贏得金馬獎。

actress
[`æktrɪs]
名 女演員

The film company contracted with the famous actress for a new project.
電影公司與那位著名女星簽了新合約。

afraid
[ə`fred]
形 害怕的

He was afraid of the ghosts even though he knew they were not real.
雖然知道都是假的，他還是很怕那些鬼。

009

高手絕招 5 補充更上一層，培養 A 級實戰力

除了必考 2000 單字，還額外編寫各式補充，例如總是寫錯的不規則動詞變化、混淆字提醒、慣用搭配詞等，英語詞彙量大爆發，絕對不只 2000 單！讓你的起跑線前移、搶分更輕鬆。

躋身會考高分群，下筆即奪 A++！

　　講到學英文的基礎，當然少不了單字。不過，無論是學英文多久的人，只要進入備考狀態，很多學生都會卡在單字這一關的輪迴出不去，不管自己背了幾千單，永遠都覺得不夠，所以單字書一本接著一本，卻始終無法撫平內心的焦慮感。

　　這次筆者根據教育部公布之 2000 英文單字，編寫本書，就是為了讓大家根除這種無止盡的恐懼感。仔細研究過去的考古題，就會發現會考的範疇不脫離這最根本的 2000 單字。若談到日常生活用語，這 2000 單字也是基本中的基本。所以，與其落入背了又忘的惡性循環中，還不如先掌握好真正會考的 2000 英單，鞏固好基礎，再往上研讀，英語實力才能真正提升。

　　國中會考的英文考科，分成聽力與閱讀兩大部分。無論考題為何，只要能抓住關鍵單字，答題就不會有問題。甚至於，近年來會刻意在考題中放入學生不認識的英文，用以考驗學生們根據上下文推敲字義的能力。

　　在考題分數的比重上，也能看出國中會考目前還是比較重視文章理解力（和聽力相比），因此，千萬不要輕忽單字的重要性，唯有熟記基礎單字，才能在遇到不認識的內文時處變不驚。

　　筆者編寫這本書的初心，無外乎是想幫助所有期望自己在會考上有所突破的考生，我們都希望自己的最終成績是「精熟」，而非讓人洩氣的「待加強」，若你也是備考生的一員，本書絕對能符合你的期待，這本書的特點如下：

一、全書內容根據教育部最新公布之 2000 單字編寫。由於歷年國中會考的出題，都脫離不了這 2000 單字的範疇，所以在編寫初期，筆者就決定以此為基礎，再逐步往上架構內文。

二、例句考量了會考 & 日常用語的平衡。基於編寫過各種英檢學習書的經驗，筆者決定以最吻合會考需求的方式去編寫例句。除了參考了過去會考的難度之外，同時也在某些例句中提升一點難度，讓考生在這 2000 單字之餘，也能掌握進階英語力，以便應對那些刻意提高難度的考題。

三、給予清楚的相關補充。像是不規則變化的動詞、相關片語 & 進階單字等，筆者都寫進了單字的補充內容中，方便讀者在觀看例句時一起學。伴隨著例句學習，再搭配本書錄製之 MP3，多聽 & 跟讀，會發現你在不知不覺中，掌握了比別人更多的英語用法。

這本書也邀請了外師錄製單字 & 例句的 MP3，強烈建議讀者搭配 MP3 一同學習，當你看著文字、聽著發音、跟著大聲讀，就能利用多種感官學習，讓你對單字的印象更深刻，再也忘不了。

本書的各種詞類整理如下：

動	動詞	名	名詞	形	形容詞
副	副詞	冠	冠詞	助	助動詞
限	限定詞	代	代名詞	連	連接詞
介	介係詞	縮	縮寫		

張翔

目 錄

Contents

MP3 01

a/an
[ə / æn]
冠 一個；某一

Brad Pitt is a famous actor in Hollywood.
布萊德彼特是好萊塢一位著名男演員。

a few
片 幾個；一些

補充 tsunami 海嘯 / a few 接可數名詞
There were a few areas affected by the tsunami.
有一些地區受到海嘯的侵襲。

a little
片 少量；一點

補充 a little 後面接不可數名詞
Sometimes you can use a little hair gel.
你有時候可以上一點髮膠。

a lot
片 大量地；許多地

Do you think a lot about the future?
你會想很多關於未來的事嗎？

A.M./a.m.
副 上午

The buffet on the first floor is served until 10 a.m.
一樓的自助餐只供應到早上十點。

able
[`ebl]
形 能夠；有能力的

補充 competition 比賽
They will judge who is able to be the winner in this competition.
他們將會決定誰才是這場比賽的贏家。

about
[ə`baut]
介 關於；大約

補充 adventure 冒險
The captain told us about his adventures of the four journeys.
船長告訴我們他四趟旅程的冒險故事。

above
[əˋbʌv]
介 在…上面；超過

The summer camp does not accept teenagers above sixteen.
那個夏令營不接受超過十六歲的青少年。

---

abroad
[əˋbrɔd]
副 在國外

補充 dormitory 宿舍
Amanda lived in the university dormitory when she studied abroad.
亞曼達在海外留學時，住在大學宿舍裡。

---

across
[əˋkrɔs]
介 副 橫越；穿過

Chris took 17 days to drive across the United States.
克里斯花了十七天，開車橫越美國。

---

act
[ækt]
動 扮演 名 行動；法案

補充 opera 歌劇 / common 普遍的
In Taiwanese opera, it is very common for women to act male roles.
在歌仔戲中，女性扮演男性角色是很常見的。

---

action
[ˋækʃən]
名 動作；行為

補充 romantic 浪漫的 / comedy 喜劇
Jenny loves romantic comedies more than action movies.
比起動作片，珍妮更喜歡浪漫愛情喜劇。

---

actor
[ˋæktɚ]
名 (男) 演員

補充 award 獎、獎品
The actor works hard at winning Golden Horse Awards.
這名演員努力地想贏得金馬獎。

---

actress
[ˋæktrɪs]
名 女演員

The film company contracted with the actress for a new project.
電影公司與那位女星簽了新合約。

---

afraid
[əˋfred]
形 害怕的

He was afraid of the ghosts even though he knew they were not real.
雖然知道都是假的，他還是很怕那些鬼。

after
[`æftə]
介 連 在…之後

補充 flee（逃走）的三態為 flee, fled, fled
The driver fled without any trace after the car accident.
車禍發生後，駕駛人逃逸無蹤。

afternoon
[`æftə`nun]
名 下午；午後

補充 confirm 確定 / appointment 會面
Please confirm the afternoon appointment with Dr. White for me.
請幫我確認下午與懷特醫生的約。

again
[ə`gɛn]
副 再一次

補充 temperature 溫度、氣溫
As the day broke, the temperature rose again.
破曉之後，溫度又回升了。

age
[edʒ]
名 年齡

Vicky looks great for her age. You'd never guess she's over 50.
就年齡來看，薇琪保持得很好，你絕對猜不到她已經超過五十歲了。

ago
[ə`go]
副 在…以前

Dinosaurs lived on Earth 230 million years ago.
恐龍生活於兩億三千萬年前的地球。

agree
[ə`gri]
動 同意

補充 terms 契約條款（使用複數形）
Do you agree to the terms of the contract?
你同意合約上的條款內容嗎？

ahead
[ə`hɛd]
副 在前方；向前

補充 與動詞搭配，可表「預先、事前」
My sister leads ahead in the racing competition.
我姐姐在賽跑中取得領先。

air
[ɛr]
名 空氣

The air pollution is getting more and more serious in big cities.
大城市的空氣汙染愈來愈嚴重。

airplane
[`ɛr, plen]
名 飛機

The two-engine airplane crashed into the farmhouse this morning.
這架雙引擎飛機今天上午撞毀了農舍。

airport
[`ɛr, port]
名 機場

We live in a place thirty-minute drive away from the airport.
我們住在距離機場三十分鐘車程的地方。

all
[ɔl]
代 一切 形 全部的

All of us need some cares from our family or friends.
每一個人都需要家人和朋友的關懷。

almost
[`ɔl, most]
副 幾乎

補充 reason 理智 / dump 拋棄
He almost lost his reason when his girlfriend dumped him.
當女友甩了他時，他幾乎失去理智。

along
[ə`lɔŋ]
介 沿著

補充 pad 步行、放輕腳步走
My father padded along the park every morning.
每天早上，我父親會沿著公園步行。

already
[ɔl`rɛdɪ]
副 已經

I've already spent too much on clothes.
我花在買衣服上的錢已經太多了。

also
[`ɔlso]
副 也

The museum is also open eight hours a day.
這間博物館一天也開放八小時。

although
[ɔl`ðo]
連 雖然

Although the hero met lots of setbacks, the end of the story is well.
雖然主角遇到許多挫折，但故事結局是好的。

always
[`ɔlwez]
副 總是

I will always think of you when I see this movie.
當我看到這部電影時，我一定會想起你。

---

am
[æm]
動 是；在；be動詞

補充 am使用於第一人稱單數、現在式

I am confused with the use of the machine.
我對於這台機器的用途感到困惑。

America
[ə`mɛrɪkə]
名 美國；美洲

補充 emigrate 移居國外

Jennifer emigrated from Ireland to America in 2020.
珍妮佛在二〇二〇年從愛爾蘭移居至美國。

American
[ə`mɛrɪkən]
名 美國人

補充 當形容詞時表「美國的、美洲的」

Peter is an American who has been living in England for over 30 years.
彼得是美國人，他住在英國超過三十年了。

---

absent
[`æbsṇt]
形 缺席的；不在場的

Steve has been absent from school for two weeks.
史蒂夫已經兩個禮拜沒有去上學了。

---

accept
[ək`sɛpt]
動 接受；答應

I offered Nina an apology yesterday, but she didn't accept it.
我昨天向妮娜道歉，但她沒有接受。

---

accident
[`æksədənt]
名 事故；偶發事件

補充 fatal 致命的、嚴重的

There was a fatal accident on the highway.
高速公路上發生一起死亡事故。

---

active
[`æktɪv]
形 活躍的

Although Ivy is over 60, she is still active in politics.
雖然艾薇已年過花甲，仍積極參與政治活動。

activity
[æk`tɪvətɪ]
名 活動

I love summer because I can enjoy lots of water activities.
我最喜歡夏天，因為可以做很多水上活動。

add
[æd]
動 增加；添加

Add some sugar into the milk tea.
在奶茶裡加一點糖。

address
[ə`drɛs]
名 地址；演說

To mail a letter, both the receiver's and the sender's addresses are required.
收件者與寄信者的地址都必須寫上，才能郵寄。

admire
[əd`maɪr]
動 欽佩；欣賞

補充 courage 勇氣 / passion 熱情
We admire him so much for his courage and passion.
我們很欽佩他的勇氣與熱情。

adult
[ə`dʌlt]
名 成年人 形 成人的

As an adult, you should be more determined and pursue your dream.
作為一名成年人，你應該要更有決心，去追求自己的夢想。

advertisement
[ædvɚ`taɪzmənt]
名 廣告

Nowadays, people are flooded by all kinds of advertisements.
現今人們被各式各樣的廣告所淹沒。

advice
[əd`vaɪs]
名 忠告

Thank you for your advice.
謝謝你的忠告。

advise
[əd`vaɪz]
動 勸告；建議

Mr. Baker was advised to have a chest X-ray.
貝克先生被建議去照胸部 X 光。

affect
[əˋfɛkt]
動 影響

補充 incident 事件
The incident did not affect the holding of the peace meeting.
這個事件並未影響和平會議的召開。

against
[əˋgɛnst]
介 反對

補充 stray 流浪的、迷路的
The town has a rule against feeding the stray dogs in public.
本鎮有規定，不准在公共場合餵養流浪狗。

aim
[em]
動 瞄準 **名** 目標；目的

補充 target 目標 / strength 力氣
To aim a target well needs the strength to hold still.
要做好瞄準，需要能維持不動的力量。

air conditioner
片 空調設備

It is impossible for us to survive this summer without air conditioner.
沒有冷氣，我們無法度過這個夏天。

airline
[ˋɛr͵laɪn]
名 航線；航空公司

You can check the timetable of the international airlines on their website.
你可以在他們的網站查詢國際航班的時間表。

alarm
[əˋlɑrm]
名 警鈴；鬧鐘 **動** 使驚慌

It is an alarm to tell us that we depend too much on energy.
這是一個提醒我們過度依賴能源的警報。

album
[ˋælbəm]
名 相簿；專輯唱片

It is popular to share your pictures with others by online album.
現在流行利用網路相簿和別人分享相片。

alike
[əˋlaɪk]
形 相似的 **副** 相似地

補充 costume 服裝
They are so much alike in the costume in the party.
宴會上穿的服裝讓他們看起來很相像。

alive
[ə`laɪv]
形 活著的；有生氣的

補充 villain 壞人、惡棍
I can't believe that villain is still alive.
我不敢相信那個壞人竟然還活著。

allow
[ə`laʊ]
動 允許；准許

補充 board 委員會 / trustee 董事
The board of trustees allowed the CEO to have a paid leave.
董事會批准執行長休有薪假。

alone
[ə`lon]
形 單獨的；孤單的

It is dangerous to be alone outside in the midnight.
半夜一人獨自在外很危險。

aloud
[ə`laʊd]
副 大聲地

補充 podium 講臺
Professor Lee stood on the podium and read the poem aloud.
李教授站在講臺上，大聲朗讀詩句。

alphabet
[`ælfə,bɛt]
名 字母

Isabella sang the alphabet song in the kindergarten.
伊莎貝拉在幼稚園唱字母歌。

altogether
[,ɔltə`gɛðə]
副 總共；完全地

補充 summit 頂峰
Altogether, there were 19 countries taking part in the summit meeting.
總共有十九個國家參與這場高峰會。

ambulance
[`æmbjələns]
名 救護車

The ambulance came several times in the neighborhood this week.
單就這星期，救護車就來了這一帶好幾次。

among
[ə`mʌŋ]
介 在…之中

Among all the musicals, *Cats* has always been my favorite.
在所有的音樂劇當中，《貓》一直是我最喜歡的。

amount
[əˋmaʊnt]
名 總數

補充 import 進口 / fabric 布料
We need to know the total amount of importing fabrics.
我們必須知道進口布料的總數量。

ancient
[ˋenʃənt]
形 古代的

This ancient house was built 300 years ago.
這棟古老的房子是三百年前建造的。

and
[ænd]
連 和；及；而

Steady exercise and healthy diet can help you lose weight.
持續的運動和健康的飲食可以幫助你減肥。

angel
[ˋendʒəl]
名 天使

補充 nephew 姪子、外甥
My nephew looks like an angel only when he falls asleep.
我的外甥只有在睡著時看起來像天使。

anger
[ˋæŋɚ]
名 生氣；憤怒

Neil took his anger out on his younger sister.
尼爾把怒氣發洩在他妹妹身上。

angle
[ˋæŋgḷ]
名 角度；觀點

補充 geometry 幾何學
He is trying to solve the unknown angle in this geometry question.
他正試著解出這個幾何題中的未知角度。

angry
[ˋæŋgrɪ]
形 生氣的

Don't be angry with him; he does not mean to cause you the trouble.
別對他生氣，他不是故意給你帶來麻煩的。

animal
[ˋænəmḷ]
名 動物

補充 feed 餵食 / wild 野生的
It is dangerous to feed wild animals.
餵食野生動物很危險。

ankle
[`æŋkl]
名 腳踝

Louis hurt his ankle when playing basketball yesterday.
路易斯昨天打籃球時傷到腳踝。

another
[ə`nʌðɚ]
形 另一個的 代 另一個

If you regret accepting this job, we can transfer it to another guy.
如果你後悔接了這份工作,我們可以把它交給別人做。

answer
[`ænsɚ]
動 回答 名 答案

Lisa did her best to answer that question.
麗莎盡力回答了那個問題。

ant
[ænt]
名 螞蟻

補充 odor 氣味 / track 行蹤、軌道
Ants find a way home by leaving their body odor along the tracks.
螞蟻靠著在路徑上留下體味,找到回家的路。

any
[`ɛnɪ]
形 任何的 代 任何一個

Are there any parking lots near the restaurant?
那間餐廳附近有任何停車場嗎?

anybody
[`ɛnɪ͵bɑdɪ]
代 任何人

Hello. Is anybody there?
哈囉,請問有人在嗎?

anyone
[`ɛnɪ͵wʌn]
代 任何人

Betty was too angry to talk to anyone yesterday.
貝蒂昨天氣到不跟任何人說話。

anything
[`ɛnɪ͵θɪŋ]
代 任何事(物)

Do you have anything to match this red dress?
你有什麼東西可以搭配這件紅色洋裝嗎?

anywhere
[`ɛnɪ,hwɛr]
副 任何地方

We couldn't get in touch with you last night. Did you go anywhere alone?
昨晚我們聯絡不上你，你一個人去了哪裡？

apartment
[ə`pɑrtmənt]
名 公寓

The family moved in an apartment with a big balcony.
那家人搬進一間有大陽臺的公寓。

apologize
[ə`pɑlə,dʒaɪz]
動 道歉

補充 scandal 醜聞

He apologized to people who had been affected by his scandal.
他向受到他醜聞案影響的人們致歉。

appear
[ə`pɪr]
動 出現

補充 It appears that...（某事）看起來⋯

The stranger appeared in this little town for unknown reasons.
那位陌生人不知為何出現在這個小鎮。

apple
[`æpḷ]
名 蘋果

Ann's mother packed a sandwich and an apple for her.
安的母親幫她打包了一份三明治和蘋果。

appreciate
[ə`priʃɪ,et]
動 感謝；賞識

補充 fortune 好運 / last 持續

Talent and fortune will not last if you don't appreciate them.
如果你不珍惜，天分與好運不會一直跟著你。

April
[`eprəl]
名 四月

補充 construction 建造

The construction of the theater will be completed by next April.
劇院的建造工程將於明年四月完工。

area
[`ɛrɪə]
名 地區；面積

補充 supply 補給品（使用複數形）

They keep delivering supplies to the remote area.
他們持續運送補給品到偏遠地區。

argue
[`ɑrgjʊ]
動 爭論

補充 trifle 瑣事、小事
Don't argue about the trifle anymore.
別再為那件小事爭論不休了。

arm
[ɑrm]
名 手臂；椅子扶手

He took the old lady's arm and guided her to her seat.
他扶著那位年長女士的手，帶她到位子上。

armchair
[`ɑrm,tʃɛr]
名 扶手椅

He sat on the armchair with his cat lying on his lap.
他坐在扶手椅上，他的貓則躺在他的膝上。

army
[`ɑrmɪ]
名 軍隊；大群

補充 badge 勳章
General Lee got a badge from the army ten years ago.
十年前李將軍從軍隊獲得一枚勳章。

around
[ə`raʊnd]
副 在周圍
介 差不多；在…周圍

The salesman took her to the house and showed her around.
業務員帶她去那間房子參觀。

arrange
[ə`rendʒ]
動 安排；整理

We arranged an appointment to discuss the possible cooperation.
我們安排了一場約，來討論可能的合作方案。

arrive
[ə`raɪv]
動 到達

When you arrive there, don't forget to buy something for Aunt Michelle.
到了那裡，別忘記買點什麼送蜜雪兒阿姨。

art
[ɑrt]
名 藝術

補充 installation 安裝 / postmodern 後現代的
Installation art is one of the forms of postmodern art.
裝置藝術是後現代主義的一種藝術形式。

artist
[ˋɑrtɪst]
名 藝術家

My best friend dreams of becoming an artist.
我最好的朋友夢想著要成為藝術家。

as
[æz]
介 以…的身份；作為
連 依照；當…時

補充 foster 領養 / orphan 孤兒
The foster parents treat the orphan as their own child.
養父母對這名孤兒視如己出。

ask
[æsk]
動 詢問；要求

When I asked the caller whether to leave a message, she hung up.
當我問對方要不要留話時，她就掛斷了。

asleep
[əˋslip]
形 睡著的

After working the whole day, she fell asleep in her chair.
工作一整天之後，她坐在位子上睡著了。

assistant
[əˋsɪstənt]
名 助手

補充 accomplish 完成
The assistant skipped a meal to accomplish the form.
助理沒吃飯以完成報表。

assume
[əˋsjum]
動 假定

Let's assume the answer is correct!
我們就假定答案是正確的吧！

at
[æt]
介 在…地點；在…時刻

The visitors are waiting for you at the gate.
訪客正在大門那裡等你。

attack
[əˋtæk]
名 攻擊 動 進攻；襲擊

補充 citizen 市民 / wound 傷害
The attack killed two citizens and wounded more than fifty people.
這場攻擊造成兩市民死亡，五十多人受傷。

attention
[ə`tɛnʃən]
名 注意；專心

What the witness said drew the **attention** of the press.
證人的證詞吸引了媒體的注意。

August
[`ɔgəst]
名 八月

Sam is planning to visit Europe to attend a conference this **August**.
山姆正計畫在八月的時候去歐洲參加會議。

aunt
[ænt]
名 阿姨；姑姑；伯母；嬸嬸

補充 smoke 燻製
Aunt Betty smoked the fish and made a wonderful smell.
貝蒂阿姨燻魚的味道聞起來很香。

autumn
[`ɔtəm]
名 秋天；秋季

補充 go sightseeing 去觀光、遊覽
Autumn is the best season to go sightseeing.
秋天是觀光的最佳季節。

available
[ə`veləbl]
形 可用的；可得到的

Do you have any dictionary **available**?
你手邊有可用的字典嗎？

avoid
[ə`vɔid]
動 避免

補充 warm up 暖身 / injure 傷害
Warming up can **avoid** injuring your waist when you dance.
暖身可以避免跳舞時傷到你的腰。

away
[ə`we]
形 不在的 **副** 遠離

The salesman is usually **away** in the daytime.
這名業務白天通常不在。

baby
[`bebɪ]
名 嬰兒

Sarah looks younger than she really is because of her baby face.
莎拉的娃娃臉讓她看起來比實際年齡小。

babysitter
[`bebɪsɪtɚ]
名 替人看顧小孩者

Serving as a babysitter for three years, Tina earns money for college.
蒂娜做了三年保姆，賺取大學學費。

back
[bæk]
名 背部；後面 副 回原處

Sleeping on a soft bed makes your back comfortable.
睡在軟墊上能讓你的背部感到舒服。

backpack
[`bæk͵pæk]
名 背包

I have a water bottle in my backpack.
我的背包裡有一個水壺。

backward
[`bækwəd]
形 向後的；落後的
副 向後；在退步

She heard a little voice and took a backward look.
她聽到窸窣的人聲，便轉頭往後看。

bad
[bæd]
形 壞的

補充 fall down 摔倒、跌倒
The lady fell down on hearing the bad news.
一聽到這則壞消息，那名婦人就暈倒了。

badminton
[`bædmɪntən]
名 羽毛球

There are some of the best badminton players in Indonesia.
有一些最棒的羽毛球選手是印尼出身的。

bag
[bæg]
名 袋子

The leather bag in the window is 120 US dollars.
櫥窗內的皮包售價一百二十美元。

bake
[bek]
動 烘；烤

Preheat the oven to 400F and bake the pizza for 17 to 20 minutes.
預熱烤箱至華氏四百度，再把披薩烤十七到二十分鐘。

bakery
[`bekərɪ]
名 麵包店

補充 anniversary 週年紀念
The bakery opened early today for its anniversary celebration.
為了慶祝週年慶，那家麵包店今天提早開門。

balcony
[`bælkənɪ]
名 陽臺

補充 ideal 理想的
A balcony will be an ideal place to put a bird feeder.
陽臺是放置鳥飼料箱的理想地點。

ball
[bɔl]
名 球

Dodge ball is a popular sport for junior high school students.
躲避球在國中生當中是很流行的運動。

balloon
[bə`lun]
名 氣球

Grandma bought me a pink balloon.
奶奶買了一顆粉紅色的氣球給我。

banana
[bə`nænə]
名 香蕉

補充 sponge 海綿
My sister has ordered a sponge cake flavored with bananas.
我姐姐訂購了一個香蕉口味的海綿蛋糕。

band
[bænd]
名 樂團；樂隊

Listening to live band alone is one of my loves.
獨自去聽樂團現場演唱是我的愛好之一。

bank
[bæŋk]
名 銀行；堤岸

補充 employee 員工

The bank laid off 50 employees last week.
這間銀行上星期裁員，解僱了五十名員工。

barbecue / BBQ
[`bɑrbɪkju]
名 烤肉

Do you want an outdoor barbecue or a formal, sit-down dinner?
你想採用戶外烤肉還是正式的桌餐形式呢？

barber
[`bɑrbɚ]
名 理髮師

補充 barber 專指替男性剪髮的理髮師

Ian is an experienced barber.
伊恩是一名經驗豐富的理髮師。

bark
[bɑrk]
動 狗叫 名 吠聲

It is unusual that a dog barked outside all night.
一隻狗整夜在外面狂吠，這很不尋常。

base
[bes]
名 基底；壘包
動 以…為基礎

補充 ecosystem 生態系統 / spoil 損壞

The base of ecosystem has been spoiled by pollution.
生態系統的根基已被汙染破壞。

baseball
[`bes,bɔl]
名 棒球

Baseball became one of Olympic sports in 1992.
棒球在一九九二年成為奧運項目之一。

basement
[`besmənt]
名 地下室

補充 emergency 緊急情況

We stored some emergency goods in the basement.
我們在地下室裡貯存了一些急救物品。

basic
[`besɪk]
形 基本的

補充 necessity 必需品

Those children lack the basic necessities of life.
那些兒童缺乏基本的生活必需品。

basket
[`bæskɪt]
名 籃子

Their baskets were filled with colorful Easter eggs.
他們的籃子裝滿了復活節彩蛋。

basketball
[`bæskɪt͵bɔl]
名 籃球

補充 sponsor 贊助者
Larry is a sponsor of the basketball team.
賴瑞是那個籃球隊的贊助者。

bat
[bæt]
名 球棒；蝙蝠

The baseball player threw down the bat after he hit the ball.
一打到球，這名棒球選手便扔掉了球棒。

bath
[bæθ]
名 浴缸；洗澡

補充 exquisite 精美的、製作精良的
Lucas bought an exquisite bath for his wife.
盧卡斯為他妻子買了一個精緻的浴缸。

bathe
[beð]
動 替…洗澡

I have already bathed the baby in the afternoon.
我下午的時候已經幫嬰兒洗過澡了。

bathroom
[`bæθ͵rum]
名 廁所；浴室

補充 mold 黴菌 / humidity 溼氣
Mold grows easily in bathrooms because of the humidity.
因為溼氣，黴菌容易在浴室滋生。

be
[bi]
動 是；要；有
助 正在…；被…

補充 date 當名詞為「約會對象」
Would you like to be my date?
你願意跟我約會嗎？

beach
[bitʃ]
名 海灘

The couple played volleyball on the beach in the afternoon.
這對情侶下午在海灘打排球。

bean
[bin]
名 豆子；豆莢

Burrito is one of the Mexican dishes made of meshed beans and flour wrap.
豆子捲餅是一種用豆泥和麵皮做的墨西哥菜。

bear
[bɛr]
動 忍受 名 熊

He can't bear that his boss shouts at him so much.
他受不了老闆這麼常對他叫囂。

beard
[bɪrd]
名 鬍子

Who is the man with a beard?
留著大鬍子的那個人是誰？

beat
[bit]
動 擊敗；打 名 節奏

補充 三態變化為 beat, beat, beaten
The king beat the servant for stealing.
國王因為僕人偷竊而打他。

beautiful
[`bjutəfəl]
形 漂亮的

You can see the beautiful scenery from the upstairs window.
你可以從樓上的窗戶看到美麗的景色。

beauty
[`bjutɪ]
名 美貌；美人

補充 makeup 化妝品 / enhance 增加
Many women enjoy wearing makeup to enhance their beauty.
許多女性喜歡用化妝品來提升容貌。

because
[bɪ`kɔz]
連 因為

Laura went to bed early because she was tired.
蘿拉很早就上床睡覺，因為她很累。

become
[bɪ`kʌm]
動 變成

補充 三態變化為 become, became, become
Why did Kate become your best friend?
凱特為什麼會成為你最好的朋友？

bed
[bɛd]
名 床

補充 spring 彈簧
The springs of the bed in the room were broken.
那個房間床裡的彈簧壞掉了。

bedroom
[`bɛd,rum]
名 臥室

There are two large bedrooms with two full bathrooms.
它有兩個大房間，和兩套齊全的衛浴設備。

bee
[bi]
名 蜜蜂

補充 sting 刺、螫（過去式為stung）
His uncle's leg was stung by a bee in the garden.
他叔叔的腿在花園被蜜蜂螫了。

beef
[bif]
名 牛肉

補充 out of 出於 / religious 宗教的
She doesn't eat beef out of religious issue.
由於宗教因素，她不吃牛肉。

beer
[bɪr]
名 啤酒

Chad was caught drinking beer by the principal in the school.
查德在學校被校長抓到喝啤酒。

before
[bɪ`for]
介 在…之前 連 以前

Hannah eats fruits before meal to keep herself from overeating.
漢娜在餐前吃水果，以免自己吃太多。

begin
[bɪ`gɪn]
動 開始

When will Jack begin his weight-control plan?
傑克何時要開始他的節食計畫？

beginner
[bɪ`gɪnɚ]
名 初學者；新手

The beginner kneed on a rock while falling from the bike.
從腳踏車跌下來的時候，那名初學者的膝蓋撞上了石頭。

behave
[bɪ`hev]
動 舉動；守規矩

Seeing her ex-boyfriend, Janet behaved like a little girl.
遇見前男友的珍娜表現得像個小女生一樣。

behind
[bɪ`haɪnd]
介 在…的後面 副 在後

補充 block 障礙（物）
There was a block behind the door. That's why I couldn't open it.
剛剛門後有個東西擋住，難怪我開不了門。

believe
[bɪ`liv]
動 相信

Do you believe that you can see your future from a crystal ball?
你相信能從水晶球裡看到自己的未來嗎？

bell
[bɛl]
名 鈴；鐘

補充 ceremony 儀式、典禮
All the church bells were ringing when the wedding ceremony began.
婚禮一開始，教堂裡所有的鐘都響了起來。

belong
[bə`lɔŋ]
動 屬於

Do you know foxes belong to the dog family?
你知道狐狸屬於犬科動物嗎？

below
[bə`lo]
介 在…下面 副 在下方

補充 warn 警告
Mother warned me that I could spend below 500 dollars a month.
我媽警告我每個月的花費要在五百元以內。

belt
[bɛlt]
名 皮帶；腰帶

The driver and passengers must fasten their seat belts first.
駕駛人與乘客必須先繫好安全帶。

bench
[bɛntʃ]
名 長凳；長椅

The old couple was sitting on the bench and watching the sunset together.
這對老夫婦坐在長凳上一同看夕陽。

beside
[bɪ`saɪd]
介 在⋯旁邊

補充 furnace 火爐

He sat on the carpet beside the furnace to warm himself.
他坐在火爐旁的地毯上取暖。

besides
[bɪ`saɪdz]
副 況且 介 除⋯之外

Besides, I want you to send me another check by Tuesday.
此外，我要你星期二之前寄給我另一張支票。

between
[bɪ`twin]
介 在⋯之間 副 在中間

補充 journal 日記、日誌

Judy liked to keep her journal between the pillows.
茱蒂喜歡把日記放在枕頭之間。

beyond
[bɪ`jɑnd]
介 超出；在⋯那一邊
副 超過

補充 endurance 忍耐

Mark pushed himself beyond the limit of human endurance.
馬克鞭策自己超越常人所能承受的極限。

bicycle
[`baɪsɪkḷ]
名 腳踏車

補充 exhibit 展示、陳列

There are sixteen different models of bicycle exhibited in the store.
店裡展示著十六台不同款式的腳踏車。

big
[bɪg]
形 大的

I want to put a big dining table in the center of the room.
我想在房間的中央放一張大餐桌。

bike
[baɪk]
名 腳踏車

補充 此為 bicycle 的簡略說法

Suddenly, Tom's bike went into a slide.
突然間，湯姆的腳踏車打滑了。

bill
[bɪl]
名 帳單 動 記入帳

補充 tear（過去式 tore）表「撕開」

Her father tore the bill into pieces.
她父親把帳單撕得粉碎。

biology
[baɪˋɑlədʒɪ]
名 生物學

補充 fascinate 迷住
My brother was fascinated with biology.
我哥哥對生物學著迷。

bird
[bɜd]
名 鳥

補充 sketch 寫生、畫素描
Joan sketched the little yellow bird in seconds.
瓊安只花了幾秒，就畫出那隻小黃鳥。

birthday
[ˋbɜθˏde]
名 生日

Abby invited all her friends to her birthday party.
艾比邀請了所有朋友來參加她的生日派對。

bite
[baɪt]
動 咬 名 一口之量

補充 動詞三態變化為 bite, bit, bitten
Molly's dog bit Lucas yesterday.
莫莉的狗昨天咬了盧卡斯。

bitter
[ˋbɪtɚ]
形 苦的；嚴酷的

I've never liked Chinese herb medicine because of its bitter taste.
因為中藥的苦味，我從來都不喜歡它。

black
[blæk]
形 黑色的 名 黑色

補充 bushy 濃密的 / eyebrow 眉毛
He's got short, black hair and bushy eyebrows.
他有一頭黑色的短髮和濃密的眉毛。

blackboard
[ˋblækˏbord]
名 黑板

Sandy drew a flower on the blackboard with a chalk.
珊蒂用粉筆在黑板上畫了一朵花。

blame
[blem]
動 責備

Do not blame yourself; it is not your fault.
不要責怪自己，這不是你的錯。

blank
[blæŋk]
形 空白的 名 空白

You need to take a piece of blank paper for taking notes.
你必須帶一張空白的紙來做筆記。

blanket
[`blæŋkɪt]
名 毯子

Sunny took a blanket to cover her feet.
桑妮拿了條毯子蓋在她的腳上。

bless
[blɛs]
動 祝福；保佑

God will bless you.
上帝將會保佑你。

blind
[blaɪnd]
形 瞎的 動 使失明

The boy became blind in a car accident.
那名男孩在一場車禍中瞎了。

block
[blɑk]
名 街區 動 阻塞

Tommy walked around the block several times.
湯米繞著這個街區走了好幾趟。

blood
[blʌd]
名 血

David lost a lot of blood in the car accident.
大衛在車禍中大量失血。

blouse
[blaʊz]
名 女用短衫

Cindy will wear a pink blouse and meet you at the gate.
辛蒂會穿著粉紅色短衫在大門口與你碰面。

blow
[blo]
動 吹

補充 三態變化為 blow, blew, blown
The wind blew away the seeds of the dandelion.
風吹走了這株蒲公英的種子。

blue
[blu]
形 藍色的　名 藍色

The blue tie matches the shirt perfectly.
藍色領帶和這件襯衫非常相襯。

board
[bord]
名 木板；車或船上；董事會

補充 proposal 提案 / director 主管
The proposal will be reviewed by the board of directors.
提案將會交由董事會複審。

boat
[bot]
名 小船

補充 inshore 近海岸的
Adam runs his fishing boat every morning to the inshore water.
亞當每天早上駕駛漁船到近海水域。

body
[`badɪ]
名 身體

We need to check all passengers' body temperature.
我們必須檢測所有乘客的體溫。

boil
[bɔɪl]
動 （水等）沸騰

Usually, it takes 7 to 8 minutes to boil an egg.
煮熟一顆蛋通常需要七到八分鐘。

bomb
[bɑm]
名 炸彈　動 爆炸

All of the bombs fell in the south part of this area.
所有炸彈都落在這個區域的南部。

bone
[bon]
名 骨頭

Generally speaking, there are about 206 bones in the human body.
一般來說，人體約有兩百零六根骨頭。

book
[bʊk]
名 書本　動 預訂

Please return all your books by the last day of this semester.
請在這學期結束之前歸還所有的書。

bookcase
[`buk‚kes]
名 書架

We need some bookcases to store these books.
我們需要一些書架來放置這些書。

bookstore
[`buk‚stor]
名 書店

補充 hang around 閒蕩
I enjoy hanging around in the bookstore and reading books.
我喜歡逛書店，在店裡看書。

bore
[bor]
動 使厭煩

I don't have any interest in government class; it bores me a lot.
我對政府管理的課程沒興趣，覺得很無聊。

boring
[`borɪŋ]
形 乏味的

The boring advertisement can't draw passengers' attention.
那則無趣的廣告無法吸引乘客的注意。

born
[bɔrn]
形 出生的；天生的

I was born in Japan but moved to Taiwan when I was two years old.
我在日本出生，但兩歲時搬來臺灣。

borrow
[`baro]
動 借入

We borrowed $20,000 from the bank to start up the business.
為了創業，我們向銀行借了兩萬元。

boss
[bɔs]
名 老闆 動 指揮

補充 boss sb. around 使喚某人
We have to give the boss an immediate reply.
我們必須立即回覆老闆。

both
[boθ]
形 兩者；兩個 代 兩者（都）

補充 score 得分 / even 同樣的
The score is even for both sides, so the last shot will be the key.
現在雙方比數相同，所以最後一球會是關鍵。

bother
[`baðɚ]
動 名 打擾；煩擾

The freckles on my face have bothered me since I was a child.
我臉上的雀斑從小就困擾著我。

bottle
[`batḷ]
名 瓶子

After drinking three bottles of wine, he became dizzy.
在喝下三瓶酒之後，他開始頭暈目眩。

bottom
[`batəm]
名 底部；屁股

No one has ever reached the bottom of the sea.
還沒有人到達海的最底端。

bow
[bo] / [bau]
名 弓；鞠躬 動 鞠躬

補充 指「弓」時，單字念作 [bo]
To play a stringed instrument, a bow is usually needed.
演奏有弦的樂器通常需要弓。

bowl
[bol]
名 碗

The bowl sets in colors are very popular in summer time.
這種彩色碗組在夏天相當受歡迎。

bowling
[`bolɪŋ]
名 保齡球

They used to play bowling every night.
他們以前每天晚上都去打保齡球。

box
[baks]
名 箱子；盒子；匣

補充 replace 取代
She selected a box of chocolates to replace the cotton candy.
她選了一盒巧克力，換掉棉花糖。

boy
[bɔɪ]
名 男孩

The boy who has curly hair is my nephew.
捲髮的那個男孩是我外甥。

branch
[bræntʃ]
名 分公司；樹枝

We will meet the manager from the Europe branch.
我們將迎接來自歐洲分公司的經理。

brave
[brev]
形 勇敢的

A brave firefighter saved the girl from a big fire.
一位英勇的消防員將女孩從火場中救出。

bread
[brɛd]
名 麵包

Bread is one of the major items in the fresh food department.
麵包是生鮮食品部的主要產品。

break
[brek]
動 打破；中斷 名 暫停

補充 三態變化為 break, broke, broken
Stephen broke the plate on purpose.
史蒂芬故意打破盤子。

breakfast
[`brɛkfəst]
名 早餐

I was running late this morning, so I skipped my breakfast.
我今天早上要遲到了，所以沒吃早餐。

brick
[brɪk]
名 磚塊

It is impossible to see through a brick wall.
要看穿紅磚牆是不可能的事。

bridge
[brɪdʒ]
名 橋

The bridge is over the River Rhine.
這座橋座落於萊茵河上方。

bright
[braɪt]
形 光亮的；明亮的

Katherine loves bright colors such as yellow and orange.
凱薩琳喜歡黃色與橙色之類的明亮顏色。

bring
[brɪŋ]
動 帶來

補充 bring the bacon home 養家活口
The husband brought the bacon home and fed the family.
那名丈夫賺錢養家活口。

broad
[brɔd]
形 寬廣的

補充 mock 嘲弄、嘲笑
The mock never bothered him because he had broad mind.
他從不在意那些嘲弄，因為他心胸廣闊。

broadcast
[`brɔd‚kæst]
動 廣播 名 廣播節目

The president's speech will be broadcast on major TV networks.
總統的演說將於各大電視網播出。

brother
[`brʌðɚ]
名 兄弟

The brother copied everything his little sister did to make fun of her.
那位哥哥模仿妹妹的所有行為來捉弄她。

brown
[braʊn]
形 褐色的；棕色的 名 棕色

補充 plump 豐滿的、胖嘟嘟的
She has a plump face with straight, brown hair.
她的臉型圓嘟嘟的，並留有棕色的直髮。

brunch
[brʌntʃ]
名 早午餐

Enjoy a nice brunch on Sunday morning is a wonderful thing.
週日早晨享受一頓早午餐，是很棒的事情。

brush
[brʌʃ]
名 刷子 動 刷

補充 dust 除去灰塵 / rack 架子
She used a brush to dust the rack.
她用刷子撢去架上的灰塵。

bucket
[`bʌkɪt]
名 水桶

He carried a bucket of soapy water to the toilet.
他提著一桶肥皂水到廁所去。

buffet
[bʌ`fe]
名 自助餐

補充 oyster 生蠔、牡蠣
Our seafood buffet includes sushi bar, fish, and oysters.
我們的海鮮自助餐包括壽司吧、魚肉和生蠔。

bug
[bʌg]
名 小蟲

I suddenly felt a bug crawling up my leg.
我突然感覺到有一隻小蟲爬上我的腿。

build
[bɪld]
動 建造；蓋

補充 elevator 電梯
They built the steps and an elevator in the park.
他們在公園裡建造了階梯和一部電梯。

bun
[bʌn]
名 小圓麵包

Tony had three buns for breakfast.
東尼早餐吃了三個小圓麵包。

bundle
[`bʌndḷ]
名 捆；大量

There is a bundle of chopsticks on the table.
桌上有一捆筷子。

burger
[`bɝgɚ]
名 漢堡

I like double cheese burger because it's delicious.
我喜歡雙層吉事漢堡，因為它很美味。

burn
[bɝn]
動 燃燒 名 灼傷

The man threw the burning paper on the ground and stamped it.
男子將著了火的紙丟到地上踩。

burst
[bɝst]
動 爆開；闖入

補充 三態變化皆為 burst
All of a sudden, the car burst into pieces.
那輛車突然被炸成碎片。

bus
[bʌs]
名 公車

Kelly, don't stick your head out of the bus window.
凱莉，請勿把頭伸出公車窗外。

business
[`bɪznɪs]
名 商業；事

補充 impressive 令人印象深刻的
Monica has an impressive business background.
莫妮卡有令人印象深刻的商業背景。

businessman
[`bɪznɪsmən]
名 商人

The businessman pushed his business to the United States.
這名商人把生意拓展到美國。

busy
[`bɪzɪ]
形 忙碌的

We took pictures of the sight of the busy city at night.
我們拍下這座繁忙城市的夜景。

but
[bʌt]
連 但是 介 除了…以外

I was planning to study abroad, but I changed my mind.
我原本計畫出國唸書，但後來改變了心意。

butter
[`bʌtɚ]
名 奶油

補充 artificial 人造的 / do harm to 對…有害
Artificial butter does harm to your health.
人造奶油對健康有害。

butterfly
[`bʌtɚ͵flaɪ]
名 蝴蝶

We found thousands of butterflies flying around us in the Butterfly House.
在蝴蝶園，有上千隻蝴蝶在我們身邊飛舞。

button
[`bʌtn̩]
名 釦子；按鍵
動 用釦子扣住

They helped the heat-stroke man undo his shirt buttons.
他們幫中暑的男人解開襯衫的釦子。

buy
[baɪ]
動 買；購買

He spends most of his money on buying computer games.
他大部分的錢都花在買電動上。

by
[baɪ]
介 透過；經由；在…之前

The package will be sent by mail tomorrow.
這個包裹明天會用郵件寄出。

Unit 03
Cc 字頭單字

MP3 03

cabbage
[`kæbɪdʒ]
名 包心菜

補充 harvest 收割、收獲
Cabbages are vegetables that harvest in winter.
包心菜是冬季採收的蔬菜。

cable
[`kebḷ]
名 纜索；有線電視

補充 steel 鋼、鋼鐵
The bridge was built with steel cables.
這座橋由鋼索建造而成。

cafeteria
[ˌkæfə`tɪrɪə]
名 自助餐館

I usually have lunch in school's cafeteria.
我通常會在學校的自助餐廳裡吃午餐。

cage
[kedʒ]
名 鳥籠；獸籠

Anna hates to see birds in cages.
安娜不喜歡看到小鳥被關在籠中。

cake
[kek]
名 蛋糕

She decorated around the cake with blueberries.
她用藍莓裝飾蛋糕周圍。

calendar
[`kæləndə]
名 日曆；月曆；行事曆

補充 lunar 月的、陰曆的
The Dragon Boat Festival is on May 5th in lunar calendar.
端午節為農曆的五月五日。

call
[kɔl]
動 喊；打電話
名 呼叫；通話

補充 client 客戶、委託人
When Julie returns, please tell her to call the client.
茱莉回來時，請她打電話給客戶。

calm
[kɑm]
動 使鎮定 形 寧靜的

My boyfriend tried to calm me down when I heard the bad news.
男友試圖在我得知壞消息時讓我冷靜。

camera
[`kæmərə]
名 照相機

As a photographer, David always carries his camera around.
身為攝影師，大衛總是帶著照相機到處跑。

camp
[kæmp]
動 露營 名 營地

Camping around a lake is a fun experience.
在湖邊露營是個很有趣的體驗。

campus
[`kæmpəs]
名 校園

Motorcycles are not allowed on campus.
校園裡禁止騎機車。

can
[kæn]
助 能；會；可以 名 罐頭

When it comes to the singer, no one can forget his deep voice.
提起這位歌手時，沒人能忘記他低沉的嗓音。

cancel
[`kænsḷ]
動 取消

If it snows tomorrow, the game will be canceled.
如果明天下雪，比賽將會取消。

cancer
[`kænsɚ]
名 癌症

補充 treatment 治療法 / breast 胸部
Dr. Yang had discovered a new treatment for breast cancer.
楊醫師已發現一種治療乳癌的新方法。

candle
[`kændḷ]
名 蠟燭

Besides the cake, don't forget the candles and a card.
除了蛋糕，別忘了還要買蠟燭和卡片。

candy
[`kændɪ]
名 糖果

Every child got a candy bag when the party was over.
小朋友在派對結束時都拿到一個糖果袋。

cap
[kæp]
名 （有帽舌的）便帽；蓋子

補充 polka dot 圓點花樣
My new cap matches my polka dot suit.
我的新帽子和圓點花樣的套裝很搭。

captain
[`kæptən]
名 隊長；機長；艦長

補充 hurricane 暴風雨 / journey 旅程
The captain never expected a hurricane in this journey.
船長沒料到這趟旅程會遇上暴風雨。

car
[kɑr]
名 汽車

One of the tires of the car is flat.
這台車的其中一個輪胎爆胎了。

card
[kɑrd]
名 卡片

Kelly boxed the shirt and put a birthday card in it.
凱莉把襯衫裝進盒子裡，還放了張生日卡片。

care
[kɛr]
動 關心；照顧

I wish you can really care about me and value my opinions.
我希望你能真正在乎我，重視我的意見。

careful
[`kɛrfəl]
形 小心的

In the summer, you have to be careful of being bitten by mosquitoes.
在夏天，你必須小心被蚊子咬。

careless
[`kɛrlɪs]
形 粗心的

A careless waiter spilt some coffee on my dress.
一名粗心的服務生把咖啡濺在我的洋裝上。

carpet
[`kɑrpɪt]
名 地毯

I don't really like our living-room carpet.
我不太喜歡我們客廳的地毯。

carrot
[`kærət]
名 胡蘿蔔

Carrots and potatoes are grown under the ground.
胡蘿蔔和馬鈴薯生長於地下。

carry
[`kærɪ]
動 攜帶；搬運

補充 forbid 禁止 / on board 上飛機
Some things are forbidden to carry on board.
有些東西被禁止帶上飛機。

cartoon
[kɑr`tun]
名 卡通

Watching too much cartoons is not good for children's eyesight.
看太多卡通對小孩的視力不好。

case
[kes]
名 案件；實例

The open case was sent to the labor union for further decision.
那懸而未決的案子被送到工會定奪。

cash
[kæʃ]
名 現金 動 兌現

Thomas never carry much cash with him.
湯瑪斯從不多帶現金。

---

cassette
[kə`sɛt]
名 卡式磁帶

Nowadays, MP3s have replaced CDs and cassettes.
現在，MP3 已經取代了光碟和錄音帶。

---

castle
[`kæsl̩]
名 城堡

補充 mysterious 神祕的
The castle is famous for its mysterious and horrible feeling.
這棟城堡因其神祕和恐怖的氣氛而聞名。

---

cat
[kæt]
名 貓

補充 grasp 抓牢、握緊
The cat jumped to the ground to grasp the fast moving toy.
為了抓住快速移動的玩具，貓跳到地上。

---

catch
[kætʃ]
動 接（球）；捕獲

補充 touch down（橄欖球）底線得分
Tom caught the ball and tried to touch down.
湯姆接住球並試圖達陣。

---

cause
[kɔz]
動 引起 名 原因；理由

The earthquake caused a power failure.
地震造成了停電。

---

ceiling
[`silɪŋ]
名 天花板

補充 chandelier 水晶燈 / lobby 大廳
A chandelier was hanging from the ceiling in the lobby.
大廳中有一個水晶燈懸吊在天花板上。

---

celebrate
[`sɛlə,bret]
動 慶祝

Today is Father's Day, so we are going to celebrate in the restaurant.
今天是父親節，我們要去餐廳慶祝。

---

cell
[sɛl]
名 細胞；單人牢房

補充 shrink 收縮
The cell will shrink once you add salty water in the glass.
一旦你在玻璃杯裡加入鹽水，細胞就會收縮。

cell phone
片 手機

補充 a variety of 各種各樣的
You can find a variety of cell phones in the store.
你能在店裡找到各式各樣的手機。

cent
[sɛnt]
名 分（美元的單位）

One hundred cents make a dollar.
一百美分等於一美元。

center
[`sɛntɚ]
名 中心（點）

You can get a free map at the information center.
資訊中心有提供免費地圖，你可以去拿。

centimeter
[`sɛntə͵mitɚ]
名 公分

She marked every ten centimeters on the cardboard for later coloring.
每十公分，她就在紙板上做記號，便於之後著色。

central
[`sɛntrəl]
形 中央的

補充 financial 金融的 / be subject to 服從於
The financial system is subject to the central control.
財政系統是由中央所掌控的。

century
[`sɛntʃərɪ]
名 （一）世紀

The 19th-century art movement was termed as Impressionism.
十九世紀的藝術運動被稱為印象主義。

cereal
[`sɪrɪəl]
名 麥片；穀類作物

補充 nutritious 有營養的
Cereal breakfast is nutritious for growing teenagers.
穀類早餐對發育中的青少年來說很營養。

certain
[`sɝtən]
形 肯定的；確實的

Danny's aim for this task is certain, so there is no need to worry about him.
丹尼的任務目標很明確，所以不需要擔心他。

chair
[tʃɛr]
名 椅子

These chairs are on sale. You can buy one and get one free.
這些椅子在特價，買一送一。

chalk
[tʃɔk]
名 粉筆

Laura wrote down the answer on the blackboard with a piece of chalk.
蘿拉用粉筆在黑板上寫下答案。

chance
[tʃæns]
名 機會

The pretty girl turned down the chance to be a model.
那位漂亮的女孩拒絕了當模特兒的機會。

change
[tʃendʒ]
動 改變；更改 名 零錢

補充 seminar 研討會 / schedule 日程表
The seminar has changed its schedule from 13:00 to 14:00.
研討會已經從下午一點改到兩點。

channel
[`tʃænḷ]
名 頻道；管道

My father changed the channel to his favorite talk show.
我爸爸將電視頻道轉到他最愛的脫口秀。

character
[`kærɪktɚ]
名 角色；特性；中文字

補充 film/movie 電影
The fans loved all the characters in the film.
粉絲們熱愛電影中的所有角色。

charge
[tʃardʒ]
動 索價；充電
名 費用；充電

The taxi driver charged the couple NT$300 for the trip.
這趟路程，計程車司機向這對夫婦要價新臺幣三百元。

chart
[tʃɑrt]
名 圖表

What does the chart tell you about the database?
這個圖表說明了資料庫的什麼內容？

---

chase
[tʃes]
動 追；驅逐 名 追逐

Can you chase that big black dog away?
能不能請你把那隻大黑狗趕走？

---

cheap
[tʃip]
形 便宜的

補充 quote 報價
The hotel manager quoted a cheaper price for them.
飯店經理向他們開了一個較便宜的價格。

---

cheat
[tʃit]
動 欺騙；作弊

補充 put down 寫下 / brief 簡短的
He put down brief notes in advance and cheated on the exam.
他事先做了小抄，在考試中作弊。

---

check
[tʃɛk]
動 檢查 名 支票；檢驗

The doctor will check Jennifer's teeth later.
醫生稍後將檢查珍妮佛的牙齒。

---

cheer
[tʃɪr]
動 向…歡呼 名 喝采；鼓勵

補充 athlete 運動員
The crowd cheered the athlete as he walked in.
當這名運動員走入時，群眾向他喝采。

---

cheese
[tʃiz]
名 起司；乳酪

補充 dairy 乳品店、製酪場
There are many kinds of cheese at the dairy.
那間乳品店裡有很多種乳酪。

---

chemistry
[`kɛmɪstrɪ]
名 化學

Chemistry was my weakest subject while I was in high school.
我念高中的時候，化學是我最弱的科目。

chess
[tʃɛs]
名 西洋棋

The puzzled game makes the chess player confused.
難解的一局令這位西洋棋選手傷透腦筋。

chicken
[`tʃɪkən]
名 雞;雞肉

Anna's mother is making curry chicken for dinner tonight.
安娜的媽媽今天晚餐做咖哩雞。

child
[tʃaɪld]
名 小孩

補充 accidentally 意外地 / comrade 戰友
The soldier accidentally killed a child and his comrade.
該名士兵不小心殺死一名小孩和戰友。

childhood
[`tʃaɪld,hʊd]
名 童年時期

補充 personality 人格、品格
Her childhood had a big influence on her personality.
童年時期的遭遇對她的人格影響很大。

childish
[`tʃaɪldɪʃ]
形 幼稚的;孩子氣的

補充 childish 為負面形容,表「幼稚」
My boyfriend's childish behavior drove me crazy.
男友幼稚的行為逼得我抓狂。

childlike
[`tʃaɪld,laɪk]
形 純真的;天真爛漫的

補充 childlike 的純真為正面形容
Anna's childlike innocence won everyone's friendship.
安娜的純真無邪贏得所有人的友誼。

chin
[tʃɪn]
名 下巴

Leo rests his chin on his hands when he is worried.
里歐在煩惱時,會用手撐住下巴。

China
[`tʃaɪnə]
名 中國

The purse you bought is made in China.
你買的皮包是中國製的。

Chinese
[`tʃaɪ`niz]
形 中國的;中國人的
名 中文;中國人

Vivian prefers Italian food to Chinese food.
跟中國菜比起來,薇薇安比較喜歡義大利菜。

chocolate
[`tʃɔkəlɪt]
名 巧克力

The chocolate store is located around the corner of the bookstore.
巧克力店在書店的轉角附近。

choice
[tʃɔɪs]
名 選擇

You should think twice before making choices.
選擇前請三思。

choose
[tʃuz]
動 選擇;挑選

補充 millionaire 百萬富翁
The millionaire chose to live in a tiny old house.
那名百萬富翁選擇住在一間狹小的老房子裡。

chopstick
[`tʃɑp,stɪk]
名 筷子

Using a pair of chopsticks is hard for a little child.
對年幼的孩子來說,使用筷子很困難。

Christmas
[`krɪsməs]
名 耶誕節

Jonathan is planning a special show for the Christmas party.
強納森正在為聖誕派對安排一個特別節目。

chubby
[`tʃʌbɪ]
形 圓胖的

補充 bear, bore, borne 生小孩
Janet had borne two chubby baby girls last month.
上個月,珍娜生了兩個胖嘟嘟的小女孩。

church
[tʃɝtʃ]
名 教堂

補充 newlywed 新結婚的人
Many newlyweds like to get married in church.
很多新人都喜歡在教堂裡結婚。

circle
[`sɝkḷ]
名 圓圈;圓形

補充 spinning 旋轉的 / illusion 幻覺
The spinning circle will create illusion if you stare at it.
如果一直盯著這個旋狀圈圈,會產生幻覺。

city
[`sɪtɪ]
名 都市

Are there any must-see places in the city?
這座城市裡面有什麼非看不可的地方嗎?

clap
[klæp]
動 拍(手);鼓(掌)

At the end of the game, everyone clapped to celebrate the victory.
球賽結束後,每個人都鼓掌慶祝勝利。

class
[klæs]
名 班級;階級

The teacher took her favorite class on a field trip to Washington D.C.
老師帶她最喜歡的一班學生去華盛頓特區校外教學。

classical
[`klæsɪkḷ]
形 古典的

They both enjoy playing instruments and talking about classical music.
他們都會演奏樂器,也愛談論古典音樂。

classmate
[`klæs,met]
名 同班同學

補充 rival 對手、敵手
Carmen took her high school classmate as her rival.
卡門把她的高中同學視為對手。

classroom
[`klæs,rum]
名 教室

補充 passage 走廊、過道
Our classroom is in the middle of the passage.
我們教室在這條走廊的中間。

clean
[klin]
形 乾淨的 動 打掃

Where are clean sheets and blankets?
乾淨的床單和毯子在哪裡?

clear
[klɪr]
形 清楚的；晴朗的

補充 gravity 重力 / manner 方式
The chapter solves gravity in a direct and clear manner.
這個章節有關重力的解釋簡潔明瞭。

clerk
[klɜk]
名 店員；辦事員；職員

補充 request 要求、請求
The customer complained about the clerk being deaf to his request.
顧客抱怨店員對他的要求充耳不聞。

clever
[`klɛvə]
形 聰明伶俐的

補充 politician 政治家 / persuasive 勸說的
To be a good politician, you have to be clever and persuasive.
想成為好政治家，必須聰明伶俐、能言善道。

climate
[`klaɪmɪt]
名 氣候

We shouldn't ignore the problems, which brought by climate change.
我們不該忽視氣候變遷所帶來的問題。

climb
[klaɪm]
動 爬；攀登

He is confident that the sales will climb up next year.
他有信心明年的銷售量會提升。

clock
[klɑk]
名 時鐘

He also repairs clocks and watches.
他也修理時鐘和手錶。

close
[kloz] / [klos]
動 關閉；結束 形 接近的

補充 announce 宣布、發布
The notice to close the shop was announced three weeks ago.
關店的通知在三週前就公告了。

closet
[`klɑzɪt]
名 衣櫥；壁櫥

The servant hung his coat in the left closet.
傭人將他的外套掛在左邊的衣櫥裡。

cloud
[klaʊd]
名 雲

補充 observe 觀察、觀測
He looked at the sky to observe the varied shapes of the clouds.
他看著天空，觀察雲的各種形狀。

cloudy
[`klaʊdɪ]
形 多雲的；陰天的

The pale light of moon was coming through the cloudy sky.
多雲的天空透出微弱的月光。

club
[klʌb]
名 俱樂部；夜總會；社團

Real Madrid is a famous soccer club in Spain.
皇家馬德里是西班牙有名的足球俱樂部。

coach
[kotʃ]
名 教練

You need a coach to improve your driving skills.
你需要一個教練來提升你的駕駛技術。

coast
[kost]
名 海岸

補充 cruise 巡航 / peninsula 半島
The sailboat cruises along the peninsula coast for scenic view.
帆船航行於半島海岸，讓人欣賞景觀。

coat
[kot]
名 外套

Put on your coat. It is snowing outside!
穿上大衣吧，外面在下雪呢！

cockroach
[`kɑk͵rotʃ]
名 蟑螂

You have to clean your kitchen; otherwise, cockroaches will multiply quickly.
你必須清理你的廚房，否則將會孳生蟑螂。

coffee
[`kɔfɪ]
名 咖啡

They had a pleasant conversation in the coffee shop tonight.
今晚他們在咖啡店聊得很愉快。

coin
[kɔɪn]
名 硬幣

補充 toss 拋、扔
Jessie tossed the coin to decide whether to join the team or not.
潔西擲硬幣來決定是否要加入隊伍。

cola
[`kolə]
名 可樂

Sam is mad because someone drank his cola.
山姆很生氣，因為有人喝了他的可樂。

cold
[kold]
形 寒冷的 名 感冒

補充 refreshing 提神的、清涼的
Cold showers in the hot summer are always refreshing.
夏天沖個冷水澡，總是令人神清氣爽。

collect
[kə`lɛkt]
動 收集

The CSI staff collected several finger prints from the crime scene.
鑑識人員從犯罪現場採集了幾枚指紋。

college
[`kɑlɪdʒ]
名 學院；大學

補充 represent 代表 / forum 論壇
He represented our college to attend the national student forum.
他代表我們大學參加國際學生論壇。

color
[`kʌlə]
名 顏色

As for the color of the dress, I prefer the blue one.
至於洋裝的顏色，我比較喜歡藍色那件。

colorful
[`kʌləfəl]
形 富有色彩的

補充 ribbon 緞帶
They decorated the living room with colorful ribbons for their mother.
她們用彩帶布置客廳來歡迎母親。

comb
[kom]
名 梳子 動 用梳子梳理

Sarah uses a comb to tidy her daughter's hair.
莎拉用一把梳子整理她女兒的頭髮。

come
[kʌm]
動 到來

You can start preparing dinner if I don't come back by four.
如果我四點還沒回來，你們就可以開始準備晚餐了。

comfortable
[`kʌmfətəbḷ]
形 舒適的

Cotton clothes are the most comfortable clothes for newborn babies.
棉製衣物對新生兒來說是最舒服的衣服。

comic
[`kɑmɪk]
形 滑稽的；喜劇的

補充 hilarious 極可笑的
He kept laughing while reading the hilarious comic book.
他讀著令人捧腹的漫畫一直大笑。

command
[kə`mænd]
動 指揮 名 命令

補充 upcoming 即將來臨的
The king commanded 2000 soldiers for the upcoming war.
為了迎戰，國王命令兩千名士兵準備出征。

comment
[`kɑmɛnt]
名 評論 動 做評論

補充 fairly 頗為、相當地
The comments from the critics around the world were fairly good.
來自全球各地評論家的風評普遍不錯。

common
[`kɑmən]
形 常見的；普通的

補充 issue 問題、爭議
The air pollution is a common issue in many cities.
空氣汙染是許多城市裡常見的問題。

company
[`kʌmpənɪ]
名 公司

The CEO of the company will come visit our factory this Friday.
這個星期五，那間公司的執行長將會來視察我們的工廠。

compare
[kəm`pɛr]
動 比較

補充 mature 成熟的
Compared with her sister, Sunny is rather mature.
跟她的妹妹相比，桑妮比較成熟穩重。

complain
[kəm`plen]
動 抱怨

I don't want to sound like I'm complaining, but it is unfair.
我不想讓我聽起來像在抱怨，但這很不公平。

complete
[kəm`plit]
動 完成 **形** 完整的

To pass the exam, you need to complete 50 questions in an hour.
要通過考試，你必須在一小時內完成五十個問題。

completion
[kəm`pliʃən]
名 完成；實現

Based on the report, work on the building is nearing completion.
根據報告，大樓即將完工。

computer
[kəm`pjutə]
名 電腦

補充 permission 允許、許可
You can't use the computer without my permission.
沒我的允許，你不能使用電腦。

concern
[kən`sən]
動 使擔心 **名** 關心的事

補充 riot 暴動 / civil 國內的、公民的
People concern that the riot would become a civil war.
民眾擔心這場暴動將演變成內戰。

confident
[`kɑnfədənt]
形 有信心的

補充 championship 冠軍稱號
The soccer team was confident of winning the championship.
那支足球隊對於贏得冠軍充滿自信。

confuse
[kən`fjuz]
動 使迷惑

You should explain more details or you will just confuse the readers.
你應該多解釋細節，不然只會讓讀者困惑。

congratulation
[kən͵grætʃə`leʃən]
名 祝賀

補充 doctoral 博士學位的
Lucy, congratulations on your well-deserved doctoral degree!
露西，恭喜妳得到實至名歸的博士學位！

consider
[kən`sɪdə]
動 仔細考慮

My brother is considering whether to accept that job offer or not.
我哥哥正在考慮要不要接下那份工作。

considerate
[kən`sɪdərɪt]
形 體諒的

It is considerate of you to drive me home after the party.
你真是貼心，派對結束後還載我回家。

contact lens
片 隱形眼鏡

Be sure to clean your contact lens every day.
要確保每天清洗你的隱形眼鏡。

continue
[kən`tɪnju]
動 繼續

補充 struggle 使勁、掙扎
She is struggling to decide whether to continue her study or not.
她正猶豫不決，不知道該不該繼續深造。

contract
[`kɑntrækt]
名 契約；合同

補充 back out 退出（計畫等）/ scheme 計畫
Ms. Smith backed out the scheme before we signed the contract.
在我們簽約之前，史密斯小姐退出了這項計畫。

control
[kən`trol]
動 控制

The government took an immediate action to control that forest fire.
為了控制那場森林大火，政府採取了緊急措施。

convenience store
片 便利商店

補充 shoplift 在店內行竊
A guy openly shoplifted from the convenience store.
一個傢伙公然在便利商店順手牽羊。

convenient
[kən`vinjənt]
形 方便的

He lives in the countryside, so the transportation is not convenient for him.
他住在鄉間，所以交通並不便利。

conversation
[ˌkɑnvəˈseʃən]
名 會話；談話

She felt bored with the empty conversation at the party.
宴會上的空洞談話讓她感到索然無味。

cook
[kʊk]
動 煮；烹調 名 廚師

Eric's mom often cooks his favorite French onion soup in winter.
艾瑞克的媽媽冬天常為他煮他最喜歡的法式洋蔥湯。

cookie
[ˈkʊkɪ]
名 餅乾

The cookies and cakes have been packaged for sale.
餅乾和蛋糕已經包裝好，可供販售。

cool
[kul]
形 涼快的；酷的 動 冷卻

The weather is getting cool these days.
這幾天天氣漸漸轉涼。

copy
[ˈkɑpɪ]
名 拷貝；副本
動 拷貝；抄襲

補充 reference 參考
You should keep one as a copy for your own reference.
你應該要留一份副本，作為日後的參考。

corn
[kɔrn]
名 玉米

The villagers here live mainly on corn and sweet potatos.
這裡的村民主要以玉米和番薯為食。

corner
[ˈkɔrnə]
名 角落

Select "my account" on the right upper corner of the web page.
點選網頁右上方的「我的帳戶」。

correct
[kəˈrɛkt]
形 正確的 動 改正；糾正

Tony wrote down the correct answer in the last minute.
東尼在最後一分鐘寫下正確答案。

cost
[kɔst]
動 花費 **名** 費用；成本

補充 transport 運輸 / afford 支付得起
The cost of the transport was too high for them to afford.
運費太高了，他們負擔不起。

cotton
[ˋkɑtṇ]
名 棉花

補充 pregnancy 懷孕
She wore loose cotton clothes during her pregnancy.
她懷孕期間都穿寬鬆的棉質衣物。

couch
[kaʊtʃ]
名 長沙發

The cat is lying on the couch in Emma's room.
這隻貓正躺在愛瑪房間的長沙發上。

cough
[kɔf]
動名 咳嗽

補充 violently 激烈地、猛烈地
The teacher coughed violently in class.
老師在課堂上劇烈咳嗽。

count
[kaʊnt]
動 數：計算 **名** 計數；計算

補充 lie on the grass 躺在草地上
Lisa lay on the grass and counted the stars.
麗莎躺在草地上數星星。

country
[ˋkʌntrɪ]
名 國家；鄉下

You'd better buy a travel guide to know the country you are going to.
你最好買本旅遊指南，了解你要去的國家。

couple
[ˋkʌpḷ]
名 配偶；一對

補充 on foot 步行
The couple went to the department store on foot.
這對情侶走路去百貨公司。

courage
[ˋkɝɪdʒ]
名 勇氣

補充 immense 巨大的、廣大的
He has shown immense courage in fighting against the enemy.
他在對抗敵人時，展現出無比的勇氣。

course
[kors]
名 課程；科目

Please make sure you attend the course on time.
上課請不要遲到。

court
[kort]
名 （網球等的）場地；法庭

Dora is a real fighter on the tennis court.
在網球場上的朵拉是一名戰士。

cousin
[`kʌzn̩]
名 表（堂）兄弟姊妹

My cousin Allen helped me to mop the floor.
我的表哥亞倫幫我拖地。

cover
[`kʌvɚ]
動 蓋住 名 封面

The path to the village was covered by the snow.
往村莊的路被大雪覆蓋住了。

cow
[kaʊ]
名 母牛

The girl got up early in the morning to milk the cow.
女孩清晨起床，替母牛擠奶。

cowboy
[`kaʊˌbɔɪ]
名 牛仔

Tom dressed like a cowboy for the Halloween party.
湯姆扮成牛仔，參加萬聖節派對。

crab
[kræb]
名 螃蟹

Autumn is the best season for eating crabs.
秋天是吃螃蟹的最佳季節。

crayon
[`kreən]
名 蠟筆

Bella brought crayons of all colors for the art class this morning.
為了今天上午的美術課，貝拉把各種顏色的蠟筆都帶來了。

crazy
[`krezɪ]
形 瘋狂的；著迷的

The mother turned crazy when her beloved daughter was dead.
鍾愛的女兒死後，那名母親就發瘋了。

cream
[krim]
名 奶油 形 奶油色的

補充 layer 層、階層
There is a layer of cream on the top of Caffe Mocha.
摩卡咖啡的頂端有一層鮮奶油。

create
[krɪ`et]
動 創造

Andy Warhol created pop art and a new style in fashion.
安迪·沃荷創造普普藝術以及一種新式潮流。

credit card
片 信用卡

Although credit card is convenient, you tend to spend more than you should.
雖然信用卡很方便，但常會使人超額消費。

crime
[kraɪm]
名 犯罪行為

The mayor proudly announced the decrease in the number of violent crimes.
市長驕傲地宣布暴力犯罪的數量有所降低。

cross
[krɔs]
動 越過；渡過 名 十字架

You need to cross the river to find the way out.
你必須穿越這條河，才能找到出路。

crowd
[kraud]
名 人群 動 擠滿

Lisa's fair skin and hair makes her stand out in the crowd.
麗莎白皙的肌膚與金髮令她在人群中特別突出。

crowded
[`kraudɪd]
形 擁擠的

補充 annual 一年一次的
The department store was crowded due to the annual sale.
由於年度特賣會，百貨公司擠滿了人潮。

cruel
[`kruəl]
形 殘酷的

補充 prisoner 囚犯
How could you be so cruel to those war prisoners?
你怎麼能對那些戰俘們如此殘忍？

cry
[kraɪ]
動 哭喊 名 哭聲

Sitting here and crying will not make any different.
坐在這裡哭一點幫助都沒有。

culture
[`kʌltʃɚ]
名 文化

補充 enchant 使入迷 / exotic 異國的
My friends were enchanted with the exotic culture of Spain.
我的朋友們都對西班牙的異國風情著迷。

cup
[kʌp]
名 杯子

They could not believe that the ball hit the cup and actually broke it.
他們不敢相信球竟然真的打破了那個杯子。

cure
[kjʊr]
動 治癒 名 痊癒

補充 symptom 症狀
Terry's symptoms can only be cured with special medicine.
泰瑞的症狀只能用專門的藥才能治療。

curious
[`kjʊrɪəs]
形 好奇的

All the readers are curious about the end of the novel.
所有讀者都很好奇這部小說的結局是什麼。

current
[`kɝənt]
形 現行的 名 水流；電流

補充 statue 雕像
The current statue was rebuilt in 1995.
現在的雕像是一九九五年重塑的。

curtain
[`kɝtn̩]
名 窗簾；舞臺布幕

Hannah parted the curtains to let the light flood into the room.
漢娜把窗簾撥開，讓陽光灑進屋內。

curve
[kɝv]
名 曲線 動 彎曲

The cliff road in curve is listed as a dangerous road.
這一段斷崖的曲道被列為危險道路。

custom
[`kʌstəm]
名 習俗

I have never heard of the custom in this country.
我從來沒聽過這個國家的這項習俗。

customer
[`kʌstəmɚ]
名 顧客

Besides basic salary, I get tips from customers.
除了基本薪資之外，我還能從顧客那領小費。

cut
[kʌt]
動 切割；剪 名 切口

Wendy cut the pizza into twelve pieces.
溫蒂把披薩切成十二片。

cute
[kjut]
形 可愛的

補充 auction 拍賣
Rose sold the cute dress by auction last week.
蘿絲上星期拍賣了這件可愛的洋裝。

Unit 04 Dd 字頭單字

MP3 04

daily
[`delɪ]
形 每日的 副 每日

There are many different trifles we have to deal with in daily lives.
日常生活中，我們必須處理許多瑣事。

damage
[`dæmɪdʒ]
動 名 損害

補充 property 財產、資產
Our property damage caused by the fire was over ten thousands.
我們因這場大火而造成的財產損失超過萬元。

dance
[dæns]
名 舞蹈 動 跳舞

Jessica had finally made up her mind to join the dance club.
潔西卡終於下定決心，參加舞蹈社。

danger
[`dændʒɚ]
名 危險

補充 extinction 滅絕
Did you notice there are many animals in the danger of extinction?
你有注意到許多動物瀕臨絕種的危機嗎？

dangerous
[`dendʒərəs]
形 危險的

Running red lights is very dangerous.
闖紅燈是很危險的行為。

dark
[dɑrk]
形 黑暗的

I turned on the light because I can't see anything in the dark.
黑暗中什麼都看不到，所以我開了燈。

date
[det]
名 日期 動 約會

The date of the party has not been set yet.
派會的日期尚未確定。

daughter
[`dɔtɚ]
名 女兒

My mother will pick up my daughter at five o'clock.
五點的時候，母親會去接我女兒。

dawn
[dɔn]
名 黎明 動 破曉；頓悟

Michael has to start working at dawn on Mondays.
麥可星期一必須從黎明開始工作。

day
[de]
名 日;白天

My skin is dry, so I use the lotion every day and night.
我的皮膚很乾,所以我每天早晚都擦乳液。

dead
[dɛd]
形 死的

補充 rescue 援救、營救
The man was dead when the rescue team arrived.
搜救隊抵達時,那名男子已經死了。

deaf
[dɛf]
形 聾的

The teenager put a deaf ear to his parents' advice.
那名青少年對父母的勸告充耳不聞。

deal
[dil]
動 處理;對付 名 交易

補充 deal with(處理)為常見片語
The boss deals with his problem by a new reward system.
老闆用新的獎勵制度處理他的問題。

dear
[dɪr]
形 親愛的

Peter was a dear baby to his grandparents.
對祖父母來說,彼得是個可愛的寶寶。

death
[dɛθ]
名 死亡

Is the death rate for stomach cancer high?
胃癌的致死率高嗎?

debate
[dɪ`bet]
名 動 辯論

They were still good friends even after the heat of the debate.
即使經過激烈的辯論,他們還是好朋友。

December
[dɪ`sɛmbə]
名 十二月

Tom and Judy are preparing for their wedding in December.
湯姆與茱蒂正在籌劃他們十二月的婚禮。

decide
[dɪ`saɪd]
動 決定

Everyone has the freedom to decide what kind of life he or she wants.
每個人都有自由,去決定自己想要過什麼樣的生活。

decision
[dɪ`sɪʒən]
名 決定

補充 crucial 重要的、決定性的
This is a crucial decision, so I need a minute to think about it.
這個決定非常重要,我需要多考慮一下。

decorate
[`dɛkə,ret]
動 布置

The designer decorated the place in brown which suits the shop.
設計師以適合這間店的棕色進行裝潢。

decrease
[dɪ`kris]
動 名 減少

補充 名詞的重音放第一音節 [`dikris]
This new medication will decrease the risk of heart attack.
新型的藥物治療會減低心臟病發作的風險。

deep
[dip]
形 深的

He took a deep breath and thought about how to explain to his girlfriend.
他做了個深呼吸,思考著該如何向女友解釋。

deer
[dɪr]
名 鹿

Bambi is a story about how a deer survives in the forest.
《小鹿斑比》寫的是關於一隻鹿在森林求生存的故事。

define
[dɪ`faɪn]
動 給…下定義

補充 define A as B 將 A 定義為 B
It's hard to define their relationship.
他們之間的關係很難定義。

degree
[dɪ`gri]
名 程度;度數

Rest the dough at a temperature of 27 to 30 degrees.
讓麵糰放一下,並將溫度保持在二十七到三十度之間。

delicious
[dɪ`lɪʃəs]
形 好吃的

補充 contain 包含、容納
The magazine contains lots of information about delicious food.
這本雜誌的內容包含許多美食資訊。

deliver
[dɪ`lɪvɚ]
動 遞送；給…接生

The furniture you ordered will be delivered this afternoon.
你所訂購的傢俱將於今天下午送達。

dentist
[`dɛntɪst]
名 牙醫

The dentist picked a few instruments and asked me to lie down.
牙醫拿了幾樣器具後，便叫我躺下來。

department
[dɪ`pɑrtmənt]
名 部門

補充 minister 部長
The minister of the Department of Health is hosting a meeting.
衛生部部長正在主持一場會議。

department store
片 百貨公司

The department store is only a few blocks away.
百貨公司就在幾個街區之外。

depend
[dɪ`pɛnd]
動 依賴

補充 distributor 批發商
We are looking for a new distributor we can depend upon.
我們正在尋找可以信賴的經銷商。

describe
[dɪ`skraɪb]
動 描述

補充 dynasty 王朝、朝代
This movie describes about the fall of the dynasty.
這部電影描述了該朝代衰敗的過程。

desert
[`dɛzɚt]
名 沙漠 動 拋棄

補充 當動詞時，發音為 [dɪ`zɝt]
In the desert, I can't see anything alive but cacti.
沙漠中除了仙人掌，我沒看到其它生命跡象。

design
[dɪˋzaɪn]
動 設計 名 圖案；設計

The clothes are especially designed for chubby people.
這些服裝是專門為體型豐滿的人設計的。

desire
[dɪˋzaɪr]
動 名 渴望

I have desired to become a soccer player since my childhood.
從小時候開始，我就想要成為足球選手。

desk
[dɛsk]
名 書桌

The information desk lies downstairs; you can go there to ask for help.
詢問處在樓下，你可以到那裡尋求幫助。

dessert
[dɪˋzɝt]
名 餐後甜點

You have to quit the habit of having brownie for dessert every day.
你必須戒掉每天吃布朗尼當甜點的習慣。

detect
[dɪˋtɛkt]
動 查出；發現

補充 investigator 調查者 / evidence 證據
The investigator detected some new evidence.
這位探員查到了新的證據。

develop
[dɪˋvɛləp]
動 發展

補充 opportunity 機會
They provide opportunities to develop students' leadership.
他們提供發展學生領導力的機會。

dial
[ˋdaɪəl]
動 撥（電話號碼）

Martha dialed me the other day and told me about her trip.
瑪莎前兩天打電話給我，告訴我她去旅行的事。

diamond
[ˋdaɪəmənd]
名 鑽石

The honest boy returned the diamond necklace to the lady.
誠實的男孩把鑽石項鍊歸還給那位小姐。

diary
[ˋdaɪərɪ]
名 日記

Keeping a diary is one of Susan's habits.
寫日記是蘇珊的習慣之一。

dictionary
[ˋdɪkʃən͵ɛrɪ]
名 字典

補充 advanced 高階的、先進的
This French dictionary is for the advanced learners.
這本法語辭典適合高階學習者使用。

die
[daɪ]
動 死；死去

Oliver's father deserted him since his mother died.
奧立佛的父親在他母親死後就遺棄了他。

diet
[ˋdaɪət]
名 飲食 動 節食

補充 go on a diet 節食；瘦身
A harsh diet does harm to your health.
太過嚴苛的節食對健康有害。

difference
[ˋdɪfərəns]
名 差別

Did you see any difference between these two paintings?
你看得出這兩幅畫有什麼差別嗎？

different
[ˋdɪfərənt]
形 不同的

補充 relative 親戚
Most of my relatives live in different cities.
我大部分的親戚都住在不同的城市。

difficult
[ˋdɪfə͵kəlt]
形 困難的

It is quite difficult to match the service this hotel provides.
要比得上這家酒店提供的服務是相當困難的。

difficulty
[ˋdɪfə͵kʌltɪ]
名 困難

This program aimed to help the students who encountered financial difficulties.
這個計畫主要是為了幫助有財務困難的學生。

dig
[dɪg]
動 挖掘

Why are you digging a hole in the middle of the road?
你為什麼要在道路中央挖洞？

diligent
[`dɪlədʒənt]
形 勤勉的

He was diligent in learning painting and finally became a painter.
他很努力學畫，終於成為一位畫家。

dining room
片 飯廳

Ms. James bought a beautiful set of cup and saucer to fit the dining room.
詹姆斯小姐買了一組漂亮的杯碟來點綴飯廳。

dinner
[`dɪnɚ]
名 晚餐

Jenny prepared a fantastic meal and invited us to dinner.
珍妮準備了豐富的餐點並邀請我們去吃晚餐。

dinosaur
[`daɪnəˌsɔr]
名 恐龍

補充 display 陳列 / fossil 化石
The museum will hold an exhibition to display the fossils of dinosaurs.
博物館將會舉辦一個展覽，來展示恐龍化石。

diplomat
[`dɪpləˌmæt]
名 外交官

補充 nominate 提名、任命
The President nominated him diplomat to Canada.
總統提名他擔任駐加拿大外交官。

direct
[dəˋrɛkt]
形 直接的　動 導演；指示

There is no direct flight service between the two cities.
那兩個城市之間沒有直航班機。

direction
[dəˋrɛkʃən]
名 方向；指示

He prays three times every day to the direction of Mecca.
他每天向麥加的方向朝拜三次。

dirty
[`dɝtɪ]
形 骯髒的

Jack washed the dirty dishes before he went out.
在出門前，傑克把骯髒的碗盤都洗好了。

disappear
[ˌdɪsə`pɪr]
動 消失

The box on the table disappeared when I came back.
當我回來的時候，桌上的箱子已經不見了。

discover
[dɪs`kʌvɚ]
動 發現

Sarah just discovered that her boyfriend was cheating on her.
莎拉剛剛發現自己男友劈腿的現實。

discuss
[dɪ`skʌs]
動 討論

The movies on the list were pretty ordinary and not worth discussing.
名單上的電影都不怎樣，也不值得討論。

discussion
[dɪ`skʌʃən]
名 討論

The discussion over the divorce was not pleasant.
離婚事宜的討論不怎麼令人愉快。

dish
[dɪʃ]
名 盤子；一盤菜

補充 roast 烤、炙 / feast 盛宴
Roast chicken is a common main dish at a Christmas feast.
烤雞是聖誕大餐中普遍的主菜。

dishonest
[dɪs`ɑnɪst]
形 不誠實的

補充 deserve 應受、該得
A dishonest person does not deserve to work for my company.
一個不誠實的人不值得為我的公司工作。

distance
[`dɪstəns]
名 距離

補充 無冠詞的 Internet 指連線的能力（抽象）
Long-distance interviews can be done by Internet.
遠距離的面談可以透過網路完成。

distant
[`dɪstənt]
形 遠的；遠離的

The museum was four miles distant from here.
博物館離這裡有四哩遠。

divide
[də`vaɪd]
動 分開；除以

補充 presentation 報告、演講
I've divided my presentation into three parts.
我將我的報告分成三大部分。

dizzy
[`dɪzɪ]
形 暈眩的

After having three glasses of wine, I felt dizzy.
在喝了三杯紅酒之後，我感到頭暈目眩。

do
[du]
動 做

補充 助動詞用於否定句、疑問句、強調句
The man is talented; I believe he can do something extraordinary.
這個人很有才能，我相信他會有一番作為。

doctor
[`dɑktɚ]
名 醫生

補充 surgery 手術、外科
The doctor gave me some medicine to ease my pain after the surgery.
醫師在手術後給我一些藥，以減輕我的疼痛。

dodge ball
片 躲避球遊戲

He would put aside his glasses whenever he plays dodge ball.
每次要玩躲避球，他就會把眼鏡放到一邊。

dog
[dɔg]
名 狗

Thanks to the aid of her friends, Jane found her lost dog.
多虧朋友們的幫助，珍找回了走失的狗。

doll
[dɑl]
名 洋娃娃

Cathy is playing with a doll in her bedroom.
凱西正在她房間裡玩洋娃娃。

dollar
[ˋdɑlɚ]
名 美元

A handmade violin could cost over a hundred thousand dollars.
一把手工製的小提琴可能會超過十萬元。

dolphin
[ˋdɑlfɪn]
名 海豚

補充 aquarium 水族館
The dolphin show is interesting and popular at the aquarium.
水族館裡的海豚秀很有趣，而且十分受歡迎。

donkey
[ˋdɑŋkɪ]
名 驢子

The farmer loaded a donkey and walked home.
農夫把貨物擺在驢背上，然後走路回家。

door
[dor]
名 門

The sweet lady held the door for the little girl.
和藹的女士幫小女孩頂住那扇門。

dot
[dɑt]
名 點；小圓點

Rita wore a dress which is black with white dots.
芮塔穿了一件黑底白圓點的洋裝。

double
[ˋdʌbl̩]
形 雙重的 動 加倍

補充 tragedy 悲劇
He's been suffering double tragedy, losing his job and girlfriend.
他最近受到雙重打擊，失去了工作和女朋友。

doubt
[daʊt]
動 懷疑 名 懷疑

Brian doubted the truth of Monica's story.
布萊恩質疑莫妮卡的故事不實。

doughnut
[ˋdo͵nʌt]
名 甜甜圈

The girl stopped when she saw the doughnuts on the shelf.
看到架上的甜甜圈時，女孩停下腳步。

down
[daʊn]
介 沿著…而下 副 向下

Walk down the street, and you will see the grocery store.
沿著這條街走，你就會看到雜貨店。

download
[`daʊn‚lod]
動 名 下載

補充 driver【電腦】驅動程式
Customers can download the driver from the website.
顧客可以從網站下載驅動程式。

downstairs
[‚daʊn`stɛrz]
副 往樓下 名 樓下

Brian ran downstairs and answered the phone.
布萊恩跑下樓接電話。

downtown
[‚daʊn`taʊn]
名 鬧區 形 鬧區的

補充 suburbs 郊區（使用複數形）
We had a difference on whether to live in downtown or suburbs.
對於要住在市中心還是郊區，我們意見不合。

dozen
[`dʌzn̩]
名 一打

A dozen of eggs cost NT$70 dollars.
一打蛋要價七十元新臺幣。

dragon
[`drægən]
名 龍

補充 symbolize 象徵 / royalty 高貴
Dragon symbolizes royalty and courage in Chinese culture.
龍在中華文化裡象徵尊貴與勇氣。

drama
[`drɑmə]
名 戲劇

Jennifer met her husband when she was at drama school.
珍妮佛在戲劇學校唸書時遇見她的老公。

draw
[drɔ]
動 繪製；描寫
名 平局；平手

補充 diagram 圖表
The salesman drew several diagrams in the sales report.
業務員畫了數張圖表在銷售報告中。

drawer
[`drɔɚ]
名 抽屜

She hid the check in the drawer of the closet.
她把支票藏在衣櫥的抽屜裡。

dream
[drim]
名 夢 動 作夢

Your dreams will come true if you work hard.
如果你奮鬥不懈，你的夢想將會實現。

dress
[drɛs]
名 洋裝 動 穿著

The bride doesn't like the style of the pink dress.
新娘不喜歡那件粉紅色洋裝的款式。

dresser
[`drɛsɚ]
名 梳妝檯

A large dresser is every girl's dream.
所有女孩都夢想擁有一個大化妝檯。

drink
[drɪŋk]
動 喝 名 飲料

In a fine afternoon, she would drink tea and chat with her neighbors.
在天氣晴朗的午後，她會和鄰居一起喝茶聊天。

drive
[draɪv]
動 開車

補充 三態變化為 drive, drove, driven
She drove for five hours without stopping to rest.
她連續開車五個小時，沒有停下休息。

driver
[`draɪvɚ]
名 司機

The brave taxi driver saved a girl from a serious accident.
這位英勇的計程車司機在一場嚴重的事故中救了小女孩。

drop
[drɑp]
動 滴落；掉落 名 一滴

The crime rate of the city has dropped two percent since his term.
從他上任之後，這座城市的犯罪率下降了兩個百分點。

drugstore
[`drʌg͵stor]
名 藥房

補充 cosmetics 化妝品
You can buy medicine and cosmetics in a drugstore.
你可以在藥局購買藥品和化妝品。

drum
[drʌm]
名 鼓

When I played the drums in a rock band, I felt very proud.
在搖滾樂團打鼓時,我感覺很驕傲。

dry
[draɪ]
形 乾燥的 動 乾燥

We know that cacti grow well in dry climate.
我們都知道仙人掌在乾燥氣候能長得好。

duck
[dʌk]
名 鴨子

The duck needs to be salted 24 hours before baking.
在烤之前,鴨肉必須先用鹽醃二十四小時。

dumb
[dʌm]
形 啞的;愚笨的

The little boy has been dumb from birth.
那名小男孩生來就啞了。

dumpling
[`dʌmplɪŋ]
名 餃子

補充 call for 需要 / ground meat 絞肉
Making dumplings calls for ground meat.
製作水餃需要絞肉。

during
[`djʊrɪŋ]
介 在…期間

During the rainy season, there would probably be landslides in mountain areas.
雨季期間,山區可能會有土石流。

duty
[`djutɪ]
名 責任;職責

補充 guardian 保護者 / educate 教育
The guardian's duty is to protect and educate their children.
監護人的責任是保護和教育他們的孩子。

each
[itʃ]
形 每個的 代 每一個

There is no sense in fighting with each other now.
現在互相爭吵一點好處也沒有。

eagle
[`igl]
名 老鷹

The eagle beat the wings and flew away.
老鷹振翅並翱翔而去。

ear
[ɪr]
名 耳朵

補充 whisper 低語、耳語
The coach whispered something in the player's ear.
教練在那位選手的耳邊低語。

early
[`ɜlɪ]
形 早的；提早的
副 早地；提早

In the early winter mornings, everything is just so still and calm.
在冬日的早晨，一切看起來是如此安定與平靜。

earn
[ɜn]
動 賺取

He started his part-time job and earned 300 dollars a week.
他開始打工，每星期賺進三百美元。

earring(s)
[`ɪr,rɪŋ]
名 耳環

補充 pearl 珍珠 / elegant 優美的
A pair of pearl earrings would make you look more elegant.
一副珍珠耳環可以使妳看起來更高雅。

earth
[ɜθ]
名 地球；土地

補充 spaceship 太空船
The spaceship will return to the earth tomorrow night.
明天晚上這艘太空船將返回地球。

earthquake
[`ɝθ͵kwek]
名 地震

A forward planning of earthquake preparation is needed for us.
我們必須事前準備好一份地震應變計畫。

ease
[iz]
名 舒適；容易
動 緩和；減輕

補充 take a nap 小睡、午睡
Sandra went back to her room and took a nap at ease.
珊卓回去她房間，舒服地小睡片刻。

east
[ist]
名 東方 副 向東方

補充 ranch 大牧場、大農場
The ranch is 50 miles to the east of San Jose.
牧場在聖荷西東方五十英里處。

Easter
[`istɚ]
名 復活節

補充 originate 發源、來自
Where did the Easter bunny originate from?
復活節兔子的由來是什麼？

easy
[`izɪ]
形 容易的

Making a joke is not easy for a serious man like John.
對於像約翰這樣嚴肅的人來說，開玩笑並不容易。

eat
[it]
動 吃

補充 三態變化為 eat, ate, eaten
The poor child hasn't eaten anything for two days.
這個可憐的兒童已經兩天沒進食了。

edge
[εdʒ]
名 邊緣；優勢

The glass rolled over the edge of the table and fell down.
玻璃杯滾到桌邊，接著掉落。

education
[͵εdʒʊ`keʃən]
名 教育

The college education turned him into a real gentleman.
大學教育把他變成一位真正的紳士。

effort
[`ɛfɚt]
名 努力；盡力

補充 animation 動畫
His effort in designing the animation won him an award.
他投注在動畫設計上的努力贏得了一個獎項。

egg
[ɛg]
名 蛋

補充 source 來源 / protein 蛋白質
Eggs are one of the best sources for protein.
雞蛋是最好的蛋白質來源之一。

eight
[et]
形 八的 名 八

Jennifer has been a secretary for eight years.
珍妮佛擔任秘書一職有八年的時間。

eighteen
[`e`tin]
形 十八的 名 十八

補充 volunteer 志願者、義工
There will be eighteen volunteers joining the rescue work.
將會有十八名義工參與這次的救援工作。

eighty
[`etɪ]
形 八十的 名 八十

This is a small elementary school and it only has eighty students.
這間小學規模很小，只有八十名學生。

either
[`iðɚ]
連 或者 代 兩者中任何一個

補充 當連接詞時會與 or 連用
Either you or I must take on that project.
我們兩個人當中，一定要有一個接下那個專案。

elder
[`ɛldɚ]
形 年長的 名 長輩

補充 take over 接管、繼任
The president let his elder son take over the company.
董事長讓他的長子接管公司。

elect
[ɪ`lɛkt]
動 選舉；選出

The president of FIFA will be re-elected in September.
國際足球協會的會長將在九月進行重選。

electric
[ɪˋlɛktrɪk]
形 電的

One thing that she treasures most is the electric guitar.
她最寶貴的一樣東西就是電吉他。

elementary school
片 小學

補充 reduce 減少、縮小
The class size of elementary schools has been reduced.
小學的班級人數已減少。

elephant
[ˋɛləfənt]
名 大象

The elephant trumpeted and scared away the hunters.
大象的叫聲嚇跑了獵人。

eleven
[ɪˋlɛvn̩]
形 十一的 名 十一

Allen has already traveled to eleven countries on his own.
亞倫已經到過十一個國家自助旅行了。

else
[ɛls]
副 其他；另外

The tour guide decided to take us to visit somewhere else.
導遊決定帶我們去拜訪其他地方。

e-mail / email
[ˋimel]
名 電子郵件 動 發電子郵件

Did you send the e-mail yesterday?
你昨天有寄出那封電子郵件嗎？

embarrass
[ɪmˋbærəs]
動 使困窘

補充 rudeness 無禮、粗野
I cannot be more embarrassed by his rudeness.
對他的無禮，我感到丟臉極了。

emotion
[ɪˋmoʃən]
名 情緒

Nina can easily understand people's thoughts and emotion.
妮娜能夠輕易地理解別人的想法和情緒。

emphasize
[`ɛmfə,saɪz]
動 強調

She used a pearl necklace to emphasize the color of the gown.
她用珍珠項鍊強調那件禮服的顏色。

employ
[ɪm`plɔɪ]
動 僱用

Schindler employed some Jewish children to save their lives.
辛德勒僱用了一些猶太兒童，救他們一命。

empty
[`ɛmptɪ]
形 空的 **動** 倒空

My stomach was so empty that I even felt dizzy.
我的肚子餓到感覺一陣頭暈目眩。

end
[ɛnd]
動 結束 **名** 盡頭；結局

補充 council 委員會、理事會
He ended his presentation with advice to the council.
他向委員會提出建議後，結束了報告。

enemy
[`ɛnəmɪ]
名 敵人

補充 missile 飛彈、導彈
The crew dealt the enemy with missiles and machine guns.
那中隊以飛彈和機關槍迎擊敵人。

energetic
[,ɛnɚ`dʒɛtɪk]
形 精力充沛的

Frank is an energetic young man.
法蘭克是個精力充沛的年輕人。

energy
[`ɛnɚdʒɪ]
名 精力；能量

補充 devote...to... 將…奉獻給…
Chris devoted his energy to teaching.
克里斯將精力投入教學。

engine
[`ɛndʒən]
名 引擎

補充 crash 墜毀 / breakdown 故障
The airplane crash was due to the engine breakdown.
這起墜機事故肇因於引擎故障。

engineer
[,ɛndʒə`nɪr]
名 工程師

補充 senior 年資深的 / technology 科技
My brother is a senior engineer of a technology company.
我哥哥是一間科技公司的資深工程師。

English
[`ɪŋglɪʃ]
名 英語 形 英國（人）的

The novel was translated to English and many other languages.
那本小說被翻譯成英文和其他許多語言。

enjoy
[ɪn`dʒɔɪ]
動 享受；喜歡

They enjoyed the last few days on the island.
他們享受在小島上最後幾天的時光。

enough
[ə`nʌf]
形 足夠的

Tony doesn't have enough money to afford the wedding ring.
東尼沒有足夠的錢買婚戒。

enter
[`ɛntɚ]
動 進入；輸入

When we entered the coffee shop, we were greeted by the sound of the piano.
一走進這家咖啡店，就有鋼琴聲迎接我們。

entrance
[`ɛntrəns]
名 入口

You will see a red sign at the entrance of the gate.
你會在大門的入口處看到一個紅色標誌。

envelope
[`ɛnvə,lop]
名 信封

補充 seal 密封、蓋印於
He signed and sealed the envelope before mailing it.
他寄信前在信封上簽名加封。

environment
[ɪn`vaɪrənmənt]
名 環境

補充 generation 世代
We should protect our environment for the future generations.
我們應該為了未來的世代好好保護環境。

envy
[`ɛnvɪ]
名 動 羨慕；嫉妒

They were looking at Danny with envy because he won the race.
他們嫉妒地看著丹尼，因為他贏得了比賽。

equal
[`ikwəl]
形 相等的；平等的

The four sides of a square are equal.
正方形的四個邊等長。

eraser
[ɪ`resɚ]
名 橡皮擦

The special eraser is designed by a famous artist.
這個特別的橡皮擦是由一位知名的藝術家所設計。

error
[`ɛrɚ]
名 錯誤

The teacher pointed out some spelling errors in my essay.
老師指出我文章中的拼字錯誤。

especially
[ə`spɛʃəlɪ]
副 特別地

The free shipping service is especially for local people.
免費運送的服務只特別提供給當地居民。

eve
[iv]
名 前夕

Spending New Year's Eve in Hawaii is a terrific holiday plan.
在夏威夷過除夕是個很棒的度假計畫。

even
[`ivən]
副 甚至 形 均勻的；偶數的

The twin sisters are so cute! They even act the same way.
那對雙胞胎姊妹太可愛了！甚至連動作都一模一樣。

event
[ɪ`vɛnt]
名 事件

補充 priority 優先 / depend on 取決於
Priority depends on how important the event is.
優先順序取決於事情的重要性。

ever
[`ɛvɚ]
副 從來；曾經

He is the most handsome movie star that I have ever seen.
他是我看過最帥的電影明星。

every
[`ɛvrɪ]
形 每一個的

My mother does exercise every day to stay healthy.
我母親每天做運動，以保持健康。

everybody
[`ɛvrɪˌbɑdɪ]
代 每個人

Everybody has to attend the meeting on Monday.
週一的會議每個人都必須參加。

everyone
[`ɛvrɪˌwʌn]
代 每個人

Not everyone can afford to study abroad.
不是所有人都負擔得起出國唸書的花費。

everything
[`ɛvrɪˌθɪŋ]
代 每樣事物

補充 destroy 破壞
The hurricane destroyed everything in this town.
暴風雨摧毀了這個小鎮上的一切。

everywhere
[`ɛvrɪˌhwɛr]
副 處處

My puppy follows me everywhere I go, even when I go to sleep.
無論我到何處，我的小狗都要跟著我，睡覺時也如此。

evil
[`ivḷ]
形 邪惡的

補充 hide 隱藏 / spell 符咒
The evil lady hid the spell under the sick man's bed.
那邪惡的女人把符咒藏在生病的男人床下。

exam
[ɪgˋzæm]
名 考試

補充 examination 的口語寫法
Sam has been preparing for the exam for two years.
山姆準備這個考試已經兩年了。

example
[ɪgˋzæmpl̩]
名 例子

補充 highlight 突顯 / strength 長處
You'd better give examples that highlight your strengths.
你最好給一些能突顯你長處的例子。

excellent
[ˋɛksl̩ənt]
形 最好的;優秀的

The excellent athlete broke the world record in his young age.
這位優秀的運動員在年輕時打破了世界紀錄。

except
[ɪkˋsɛpt]
介 除…之外

補充 out of stock 無庫存
The sizes of the shoes are out of stock, except for the twenty-four.
這雙鞋的尺寸都沒貨了,只有二十四號還有。

excite
[ɪkˋsaɪt]
動 使興奮;使激動

補充 supporter 支持者
The news of the victory excites the team's supporters.
獲勝的消息使這一隊的支持者激動不已。

excited
[ɪkˋsaɪtɪd]
形 感到興奮的

The prize-winning actress was too excited to speak.
得獎的女演員興奮得說不出話。

exciting
[ɪkˋsaɪtɪŋ]
形 令人興奮的

It is an exciting moment that the host is going to draw the biggest prize.
這是令人興奮的一刻,主持人將要抽出大獎。

excuse
[ɪkˋskjuz]
動 原諒 名 藉口

Please excuse me for leaving early this afternoon.
請原諒我今天下午要早退。

exercise
[ˋɛksɚˏsaɪz]
名 運動;習題

Do a little exercise every day will make you happy and healthy.
每天做一點運動會讓你快樂又健康。

exist
[ɪg`zɪst]
動 存在

補充 no longer 不再
Dinosaurs no longer exist on Earth.
恐龍已經不存在於地球。

exit
[`ɛksɪt]
名 出口 **動** 離開

Several people were burnt alive because the exit was blocked.
由於出口被堵住，好幾個人被活活燒死。

expect
[ɪk`spɛkt]
動 期待

I did not expect you to be on time this afternoon.
我沒想到今天下午你會準時。

expensive
[ɪk`spɛnsɪv]
形 昂貴的

補充 usual 通常的、平常的
All-Star Game Tickets are always more expensive than usual.
全明星賽的門票總是比一般比賽昂貴。

experience
[ɪk`spɪrɪəns]
名 經驗 **動** 經歷；感受到

補充 biotechnology 生物工程 / industry 工業
Chris has years of experience in the biotechnology industry.
克里斯在生化科技產業裡有多年的經歷。

explain
[ɪk`splen]
動 解釋

Although we explained over and over again, Ann did not get it.
雖然我們一再解釋，安仍然搞不懂。

express
[ɪk`sprɛs]
動 表達 **名** 快遞；快車

Don't be shy while expressing your opinions.
表達你的意見時不要害羞。

extra
[`ɛkstrə]
形 額外的
名 額外的人或錢財

補充 newcomer 新手 / keep up with 趕上
The newcomer made extra efforts to keep up with others.
為了趕上其他人，那名新手付出了額外的努力。

eye
[aɪ]
名 眼睛

The baby rolled her eyes, looking at people around her.
小嬰兒眼睛骨碌碌地轉，看向她周圍的人群。

face
[fes]
名 臉 動 面對

補充 burst out 突然…起來（接動名詞）
I burst out laughing when I saw Tommy's funny face.
一看見湯米的鬼臉，我就大笑出聲。

fact
[fækt]
名 事實

In fact, Mr. White is not the right person for this position.
事實上，懷特先生不是這個職位的最佳人選。

factory
[`fæktərɪ]
名 工廠

When I was your age, I had to work in a factory.
我在你這個年齡時必須去工廠工作。

fail
[fel]
動 失敗；不及格

補充 upset 心煩的
He is very upset for he failed to complete the project.
由於沒有完成這項專案，他感到非常沮喪。

fair
[fɛr]
形 公平的；美好的

Ivy got a fair price to buy the house.
艾薇以公平合理的價格買了那間房子。

fall
[fɔl]
動 落下 名 秋季

補充 三態變化為 fall, fell, fallen
This morning, Claire fell from the bike and hurt her ankle.
克萊兒早上從腳踏車摔下來，弄傷了腳踝。

false
[fɔls]
形 錯誤的；假的

補充 accuse 控告
The actor decided to accuse the media for the false report.
由於不實的報導，那位演員決定控告報社。

family
[`fæməlɪ]
名 家庭

Everyone in my family likes different kinds of musical instruments.
我家裡每個人喜歡的樂器都不同。

famous
[`feməs]
形 著名的

My aunt, Molly, is a successful and famous scientist.
我阿姨莫莉是位既成功又著名的科學家。

fan
[fæn]
名 電風扇；粉絲

Fans gathered outside the hall to see the sports star.
球迷聚集在大廳外，爭睹那名球星的風采。

fancy
[`fænsɪ]
形 花俏的；別緻的

Samantha loves fancy clothes and shoes.
莎曼珊喜歡別緻的衣服與鞋子。

fantastic
[fæn`tæstɪk]
形 奇妙的

補充 casino 賭場
Robert was in fantastic luck and won an amount of money in the casino.
羅伯特的運氣太驚人，在賭場贏了一筆錢。

far
[fɑr]
形 遙遠的 副 遠方地

補充 clinic 診所
The clinic Joe wants to go to is very far; he should look for a closer one.
喬想去的診所非常遠，他應該找比較近的。

farm
[fɑrm]
名 農場 動 務農

補充 acre 英畝
My uncle's farm is five thousand acres.
我叔叔的農場有五千英畝。

farmer
[`fɑrmɚ]
名 農夫

補充 be worried about 擔心
Farmers are worried about the coming typhoon.
農夫擔心著即將來襲的颱風。

fashionable
[`fæʃənəbḷ]
形 時尚的

It became fashionable to wear big sunglasses.
戴上大太陽眼鏡後就變得很時髦。

fast
[fæst]
形 快速的 副 很快地

補充 reliable 可靠的
Mail is public service and it needs to be fast and reliable.
郵政是公眾服務，必須快速可靠。

fat
[fæt]
形 胖的

補充 regularly 有規律地、定期地
Lisa exercises regularly, so she never gets fat.
麗莎很規律地運動，所以她不曾發福。

father
[`fɑðɚ]
名 父親

Professor Wu is the greatest father that I have ever seen.
吳教授是我見過最偉大的父親。

faucet
[`fɔsɪt]
名 水龍頭

The kid turned on the faucet to wash his hands.
那個孩子打開水龍頭洗手。

fault
[fɔlt]
名 過錯

補充 admit 承認
Patrick admitted it was his fault and apologized.
派翠克承認是他的錯，並道歉。

favorite
[`fevərɪt]
形 最喜愛的

Modern history is my favorite subject in college.
在大學裡，我最喜歡的科目是現代歷史。

fear
[fɪr]
名 懼怕 動 畏懼

補充 fight against 與⋯對抗、作戰
The boy fought against the bad guys without fear.
那名男孩毫無畏懼地與壞人對抗。

February
[`fɛbru͵ɛrɪ]
名 二月

We will have been together for ten years by next February.
到了明年二月，我們就在一起十年了。

fee
[fi]
名 費用

I didn't have much money left after I paid the doctor's fee.
付完診療費後，我沒剩多少錢了。

feed
[fid]
動 餵養

My sister feeds her cats twice a day.
我姐姐一天餵她的貓兩次。

feel
[fil]
動 感覺

Danny felt the house shake, so he ran out immediately.
丹尼覺得屋子在震動，所以他立刻跑出去。

female
[`fimel]
名 女性 形 女性的

補充 hot spring 溫泉
The hot spring on the right side is for females only.
右邊的溫泉僅供女性使用。

fence
[fɛns]
名 柵欄；籬笆

The old lady talked to her neighbors over the fence.
那名年邁的女士和鄰居隔著籬笆聊天。

festival
[`fɛstəvḷ]
名 節日

The Moon Festival is a unique national holiday to us.
中秋節對我們而言,是很獨特的節日。

---

fever
[`fivɚ]
名 發燒

補充 take a day off 請一天假 / slight 輕微的
James took a day off because he got a slight fever.
詹姆士有點發燒,所以他請了一天假。

---

few
[fju]
形 少數的 代 少數

補充 與 a 連用的 a few 表示「一些」
The dormitory is just a few steps away from the campus.
宿舍離校園僅有幾步路的距離。

---

fifteen
[`fɪf`tin]
形 十五的 名 十五

補充 suitable 合適的、適宜的
The movie is not suitable for teenagers who are under fifteen.
這部電影不適合未滿十五歲的青少年觀看。

---

fifty
[`fɪftɪ]
形 五十的 名 五十

The bagel was on sale at the price of fifty cents each after nine.
九點以後,貝果麵包會有促銷,每個賣五角。

---

fight
[faɪt]
動 打架;作戰
名 打架;戰爭

補充 boxer 拳擊手 / opponent 對手
The boxer has fought five opponents.
這名拳擊手已和五位對手搏鬥過。

---

file
[faɪl]
名 檔案;案卷 動 把…歸檔

The professor needs twenty copies of this file.
教授需要二十份這個檔案的拷貝。

---

fill
[fɪl]
動 充滿;填滿

補充 fill in 填寫
Please check if there is any information you didn't fill in.
請檢查一下,你是否有資料沒有填寫。

film
[fɪlm]
名 電影；影片

The production cost of making the film was too high.
電影的製作成本太高了。

final
[`faɪn!]
形 最終的

The character died in the final scene of this play.
在這齣戲的最後一幕，這個角色逝世了。

find
[faɪnd]
動 找到

補充 三態變化為 find, found, found
The children finally found the way home.
那群孩子們最後終於找到回家的路。

fine
[faɪn]
形 好的；優秀的

France is among the most famous places where fine red wine is produced.
論頂級紅酒，法國是世界知名的產地之一。

finger
[`fɪŋgɚ]
名 手指

補充 cook 廚師 / slice 切成薄片
The cook cut his finger while slicing pork this morning.
這名廚師早上切豬肉時切到手指。

finish
[`fɪnɪʃ]
動 完成

補充 assignment 作業、任務
You should go back to finish your assignment first. We'll meet later.
你應該先回去把作業寫完，我們晚點再碰面。

fire
[`faɪr]
名 火 動 開炮；解僱

補充 crew 一組人員 / barn 農舍
When the fire crew arrived, the house and the barn were burning.
消防員抵達時，房子與農舍已陷入火海。

first
[fɝst]
形 第一的

補充 dress up 裝扮 / gown 女禮服
The first lady dressed herself up in a classical white gown.
第一夫人以經典的白色長禮服裝扮自己。

fish
[fɪʃ]
名 魚 動 釣魚

補充 peddler 小販 / live 活的
The peddler sells live fish in the market every day.
小販每天在市場販賣活魚。

fisherman
[`fɪʃəmən]
名 漁夫

The fisherman didn't notice the coming of the storm.
那位漁夫沒注意到暴風雨即將到來。

fit
[fɪt]
動 合身；適合

This pair of sunglasses fit Tony well.
這副太陽眼鏡很適合東尼。

five
[faɪv]
形 五的 名 五

We were assigned a rush job which needs to be done in five hours.
我們突然被指派了一份緊急任務，要在五個小時之內完成。

fix
[fɪks]
動 修理

His father fixed the bike's handle for him on Saturday.
星期六他父親替他修理了腳踏車的把手。

flag
[flæg]
名 旗子

The player raised the national flag on the awarding ceremony.
那名選手在頒獎典禮上舉起國旗。

flashlight
[`flæʃ,laɪt]
名 手電筒

補充 blackout 停電
In a blackout night, you'll need a flashlight.
在停電的夜晚，你會需要一支手電筒。

flat tire
片 爆胎

When Sunny got back, she found the flat tire of her new car.
當桑妮回來時，發現她的新車爆胎了。

flight
[flaɪt]
名 飛行；班機

The flight is canceled because of engine trouble.
航班因為引擎故障而取消了。

floor
[flor]
名 地板；樓

補充 wooden 木製的
They painted the wooden floor white.
他們將木地板漆成了白色。

flour
[flaʊr]
名 麵粉

The price of flour has been raised by 20% during this month.
麵粉的價格在這個月已漲了百分之二十。

flower
[`flaʊɚ]
名 花

補充 pack 將…擠滿
In the flower season, the city would be packed with visitors.
花季一到，這個城市就會擠滿遊客。

flu
[flu]
名 流行性感冒

補充 latest 最新的 / quarantine 隔離
The patients who caught the latest flu have to be quarantined.
感染最新流行性感冒的病患必須被隔離起來。

flute
[flut]
名 長笛；橫笛

The girl plays the flute while I'm playing guitar.
我彈吉他的時候，那名女孩負責吹長笛。

fly
[flaɪ]
動 飛 名 蒼蠅

補充 goose 鵝（複數形為 geese）
I don't know why geese cannot fly with their wings.
我不懂為何鵝有翅膀卻飛不起來。

focus
[`fokəs]
動 集中 名 焦點

補充 ability 能力 / appearance 外貌
You should focus more on your ability, not on your appearance.
你應該多注重你的能力，而非外表。

fog
[fɑg]
名 霧

Those tourists got lost because of the heavy fog.
那群遊客因濃霧而迷了路。

foggy
[`fɑgɪ]
形 有霧的；多霧的

My grandfather lived in a foggy city near the mountains.
我祖父住在靠山區的一個多霧城市。

follow
[`fɑlo]
動 跟隨；遵循

We followed her up the steps and walked into a grand hall.
我們跟著她爬上樓梯，走進一個宏偉寬敞的大廳。

food
[fud]
名 食物

Dora spends $3000 on pet food every month.
朵拉每個月花在寵物糧食上的費用約三千元。

fool
[ful]
名 傻子 動 愚弄

Ben is a fool if he believes Jessica's excuse.
如果班相信潔西卡的藉口，那他就是傻子。

foolish
[`fulɪʃ]
形 愚笨的

How foolish am I to fall in love with someone like him?
我怎麼會傻到愛上他這樣的人？

foot
[fʊt]
名 腳；英尺

Little Daisy likes to put her feet in the swimming pool.
小黛西喜歡把腳放進游泳池中。

football
[`fʊt͵bɔl]
名 美式橄欖球

Football is one of the most popular sports in the U.S.
橄欖球在美國是最受歡迎的運動之一。

for
[fɔr]
介 為了；往 連 因為；由於

補充 patriot 愛國者 / shed 流出
Patriots would shed blood for their country.
愛國者會為國家灑熱血。

foreign
[`fɔrɪn]
形 外國的；外來的

He visited many foreign countries to experience new things.
他走訪許多國家以體驗新事物。

foreigner
[`fɔrɪnɚ]
名 外國人

補充 tutor 指導、輔導
The teacher tutored the foreigner in Chinese.
這位老師輔導這名外國人學中文。

forest
[`fɔrɪst]
名 森林

Do you know how many houses were burned down because of the forest fire?
你知道這場森林大火燒毀了多少房子嗎？

forget
[fɚ`gɛt]
動 忘記

補充 三態變化為 forget, forgot, forgotten
Billy forgot his camera in the cab.
比利把相機忘在計程車上了。

forgive
[fɚ`gɪv]
動 原諒

At the last moment, the man chose to forgive his parents.
在最後一刻，男子選擇原諒他的父母。

fork
[fɔrk]
名 叉子

補充 courtesy 禮貌
It is a courtesy not to make noises by the fork when dining.
吃東西時，不讓叉子發出聲響是一種禮貌。

form
[fɔrm]
動 形成 名 形式；表格

A hurricane formed 300 miles off the west coast of Mexico.
墨西哥西岸三百英里處有一個颶風形成。

formal
[`fɔrml]
形 正式的

They promised me a job, but I haven't received a formal contract yet.
他們承諾會給我一份工作，但我尚未收到正式的合約。

former
[`fɔrmɚ]
形 前者的；前任的

The former president of this country is not welcomed.
這個國家的前總統不受歡迎。

forty
[`fɔrtɪ]
形 四十的 名 四十

From her appearance and dressing, she is probably in her early forties.
從外貌與穿著打扮來看，她應該四十出頭。

forward
[`fɔrwəd]
副 向前 形 前面的 動 轉交

補充 creep 爬行、匍匐而行
They crept forward under the smoke and the fire.
他們在煙霧與火焰的籠罩下向前爬行。

four
[for]
形 四的 名 四

Rick has been sitting there for almost four hours. What is he reading?
瑞克坐在那裡將近四小時了，他在讀什麼？

fourteen
[`for`tin]
形 十四的 名 十四

It is hard to believe that he has a fourteen year-old daughter.
很難相信他已經有個十四歲的女兒。

fox
[fɑks]
名 狐狸

補充 burrow 挖洞穴 / bush 灌木叢
The fox burrowed a hole near the bush.
那隻狐狸在灌木叢附近挖了一個洞。

frank
[fræŋk]
形 坦白的

補充 qualified 合格的、勝任的
To be frank, Karen is not qualified for this job.
老實說，凱倫沒有達到這份工作的標準。

free
[fri]
形 免費的；自由的

If you buy three books today, you can get one free mug.
如果你今天買三本書，就可以免費獲得一個馬克杯。

freedom
[`fridəm]
名 自由

補充 fate 命運
We have the freedom to decide our own fate.
我們有決定自己命運的自由。

freezer
[`frizɚ]
名 冰箱的冷凍庫

You should put meat and fish in the freezer.
你應該把肉類與魚類放進冷凍庫。

freezing
[`frizɪŋ]
形 冰凍的；極冷的

I closed the window because it was freezing there.
那裡冷極了，所以我把窗戶關上。

French
[frɛntʃ]
形 法國的；法語的
名 法國人；法語

補充 Vietnam 越南 / colony 殖民地
Vietnam was once a French colony.
越南曾是法國的殖民地。

French fries
片 薯條

He had two cheese burgers and three packets of French fries.
他吃了兩個吉事漢堡和三包薯條。

fresh
[frɛʃ]
形 新鮮的

補充 port 港口
Fu-chi fishing port is a good place to taste fresh seafood.
富基漁港是個品嚐新鮮海產的好地方。

Friday
[`fraɪˌde]
名 星期五

I had a wonderful night on Friday, but the hangover was killing me.
我度過絕妙的週五夜晚，但宿醉太痛苦了。

fridge
[frɪdʒ]
名【口】冰箱

補充 為口語用法，完整英文為 refrigerator
Can you bring me some ice cubes from the fridge?
你可以從冰箱拿一些冰塊給我嗎？

friend
[frɛnd]
名 朋友

Vicky left her kitten to her best friend when she was away.
薇琪不在的時候，把小貓交給她的好友照顧。

friendly
[`frɛndlɪ]
形 友善的

補充 get used to 漸漸習慣於
The friendly trainer helped me get used to the work.
那名友善的訓練員幫助我熟悉工作。

friendship
[`frɛndʃɪp]
名 友誼

Joe and Sam's friendship started from the kindergarten.
喬和山姆的友誼從幼稚園時開始建立。

frighten
[`fraɪtṇ]
動 害怕；驚恐

Many children are frightened by the toy monster.
許多小孩都被玩具怪物嚇到了。

Frisbee
[`frɪzbi]
名 飛盤

補充 由於是廠牌名，所以使用時 F 需大寫
We saw a lot of people playing Frisbee in the park.
我們看到許多人在公園玩飛盤。

frog
[frɑg]
名 青蛙

補充 scream 尖叫
Tracy screamed when she saw the frog on her table.
一看見她桌上的青蛙，崔西便尖叫起來。

from
[frɑm]
介 從；始於

If you take the pillow away from the baby, he would wake up.
如果把枕頭從嬰兒身邊拿走，他就會醒來。

front
[frʌnt]
名 前方　形 前面的

補充 mansion 大廈、大樓
There is a big garden in front of their mansion.
他們的大樓前面有個很大的花園。

fruit
[frut]
名 水果

補充 order 訂單（這裡當名詞使用）
Every order of our juice is made of fresh fruit.
我們的果汁都是用新鮮水果打的。

fry
[fraɪ]
動 油炸

To prepare the meal, he fried the eggs and chopped the vegetables.
為了準備餐點，他煎了蛋，並切好蔬菜。

full
[fʊl]
形 飽的；滿的

補充 be full of 充滿⋯的
The relationship between Frank and Tina is full of drama.
法蘭克與蒂娜之間的關係很戲劇化。

fun
[fʌn]
名 樂趣

Thank you for inviting me. I had a lot of fun today.
謝謝你的邀請，我今天玩得很高興。

funny
[`fʌnɪ]
形 可笑的；滑稽的

The host started the show with a funny joke.
作為節目開場，主持人說了個滑稽的笑話。

furniture
[`fɜnɪtʃɚ]
名 傢俱

This apartment without furniture is for rent.
這間公寓正在出租，不含傢俱。

future
[`fjutʃɚ]
名 未來　形 未來的

I think that our future is determined by ourselves.
我認為命運是由自己決定的。

gain
[gen]
動 得到；獲得

Tony formed a habit of reading and gained knowledge from it.
東尼養成了讀書的習慣，得到不少知識。

game
[gem]
名 比賽；遊戲

The game is quite intense. Our team is one point behind now.
這場比賽競爭相當激烈，我們的隊伍現在落後敵隊一分。

garage
[gə`raʒ]
名 車庫

補充 abandon 丟棄 / workshop 作坊
The abandoned garage used to be the man's workshop.
那間廢棄車庫曾是那名男人的工作室。

garbage
[`garbɪdʒ]
名 垃圾

He took out two bags of garbage from the kitchen.
他從廚房拿出兩袋垃圾。

garden
[`gardṇ]
名 花園

My mother grew many lilies in the garden last month.
我母親上個月在花園裡種了很多百合。

gas
[gæs]
名 汽油；瓦斯

補充 fork 分歧、分岔
Before the gas station, the path forks in two directions.
加油站前的道路岔成兩個方向。

gate
[get]
名 柵門；登機門

After discussing with the designer, Kyle painted his gate red.
在與設計師討論之後，凱爾將他家的大門漆成紅色。

gather
[`gæðɚ]
動 集合

Leaders of the world gathered together to discuss about the issue.
世界領袖齊聚一堂，討論這個議題。

general
[`dʒɛnərəl]
形 普遍的 **名** 將軍

Patrick explained the general idea of his proposal.
針對他的提案，派翠克說明了大概的想法。

generous
[`dʒɛnərəs]
形 慷慨的

She is generous to those who have financial difficulty.
她對那些財務有困難的人相當慷慨。

genius
[`dʒinjəs]
名 天才

Albert Einstein is a well-known genius.
愛因斯坦是眾所皆知的天才。

gentle
[`dʒɛntḷ]
形 溫柔的

補充 weep 哭泣、流淚 / comfort 安慰
The weeping child was comforted by Joey's gentle voice.
哭泣的孩子因喬伊溫柔的嗓音而得到安慰。

gentleman
[`dʒɛntḷmən]
名 紳士

補充 portrait 肖像
There is a portrait of an English gentleman hanging on the wall.
牆上掛著一位英國紳士的肖像畫。

geography
[dʒi`agrəfi]
名 地理

My favorite subject in high school was geography.
我高中時最喜歡的科目就是地理。

gesture
[`dʒɛstʃɚ]
名 手勢 **動** 打手勢

I don't understand what that gesture means.
我不懂那個手勢的意思。

get
[gɛt]
動 獲得；得到

He cannot get a better price on this business deal.
針對這筆生意，他無法取得更好的價格。

ghost
[gost]
名 鬼

You should not scare the kid with ghost stories.
你不應該用鬼故事嚇小孩。

giant
[`dʒaɪənt]
形 巨大的 名 巨人

補充 sculpture 雕像
It is hard to ship such a giant sculpture overseas.
越洋運送如此巨大的雕塑品很困難。

gift
[gɪft]
名 禮物

The toy gun is a gift from his grandfather.
這把玩具槍是他爺爺送的。

girl
[gɜl]
名 女孩

補充 own 擁有
That girl dreams of owning a coffee shop.
那名女孩夢想擁有一間咖啡廳。

give
[gɪv]
動 給予

補充 三態變化為 give, gave, given
For his hard work, the boss gave him a long vacation.
因為他的勤奮，老闆給了他一個長假。

glad
[glæd]
形 高興的

補充 bump into 巧遇、偶遇
I'm really glad that we bumped into each other.
我真的很高興我們能遇見彼此。

glass
[`glæs]
名 玻璃杯；玻璃

補充 toast 舉杯祝酒
Let's raise our wine glasses and toast to our host.
讓我們舉起酒杯，向主人敬酒。

glasses
[`glæsɪz]
名 眼鏡

With the glasses of white frame, she certainly made a unique image.
戴著白框眼鏡，她確實打造出獨特形象。

glove
[glʌv]
名 手套

補充 通常會搭配 a pair of（一雙）使用
He put on a pair of white cotton gloves and then took out the vase.
他戴上一副白色棉手套，接著拿出花瓶。

glue
[glu]
動 黏住；緊附 名 膠水

She glued the broken pieces together for all night.
她整晚都在把碎片一一黏牢。

go
[go]
動 去；走

補充 三態變化為 go, went, gone
We went to see a play, which is adapted from Shakespeare's script.
我們去看了一齣改編自莎士比亞劇本的戲劇。

goal
[gol]
名 目標；球門

She is the first one who reached monthly sales goal for months.
幾個月來，她是第一個達成月銷量目標的人。

goat
[got]
名 山羊

補充 flock（牲畜等的）群
The little girl was excited when she saw a flock of goats.
看到一群山羊的小女孩顯得很興奮。

god
[gɑd]
名 上帝

補充 當「上帝」解釋時需大寫
Do you believe in God?
你信仰上帝嗎？

gold
[gold]
名 黃金 形 金製的

Gold is a kind of precious metals.
金子是一種貴重金屬。

golden
[`goldn]
形 金色的

The king wore a golden crown in symbol of his greatness.
國王戴了一頂金色皇冠來彰顯他的偉大。

---

golf
[gɑlf]
名 高爾夫球

My father plays golf every Saturday morning.
我爸爸每個星期六早上都去打高爾夫球。

---

good
[gʊd]
形 好的

補充 be good at 擅長某事
The photographer is good at taking photos of landscapes.
這名攝影師擅長拍攝風景照。

---

goodbye
[ˌgʊd`baɪ]
名 再見；再會

Saying goodbye is never easy for me.
道別對我而言並不容易。

---

goose
[gus]
名 鵝

We had honey roasted goose for lunch.
我們午餐吃蜜汁烤鵝。

---

government
[`gʌvənmənt]
名 政府

The government should try to create more job opportunities.
政府應該創造更多的就業機會。

---

grade
[gred]
名 分數；年級

補充 right 權利（名詞）
You have the right to check your grade within two weeks.
你有權在兩個星期內查詢成績。

---

gram
[græm]
名 公克

補充 intake 吸收、攝取
A healthy daily intake of salt is less than six grams.
為維持健康，每日鹽的攝取量應低於六公克。

granddaughter
[`græn,dɔtɚ]
名 孫女；外孫女

Do you know who Amy's granddaughter is?
你知道艾咪的孫女是誰嗎？

---

grandfather
[`græn,faðɚ]
名 爺爺；外公

補充 stick 手杖、棍子
My grandfather needs a stick to support him while walking.
我的爺爺走路時需要拐杖的支撐。

---

grandmother
[`græn,mʌðɚ]
名 奶奶；外婆

The necklace my grandmother left me is very valuable.
祖母留給我的項鍊很有價值。

---

grandson
[`græn,sʌn]
名 孫子；外孫

Mr. Evans left all his money to his grandson.
埃文斯先生將他所有的錢留給了孫子。

---

grape
[grep]
名 葡萄

補充 shoot 幼芽、幼枝
Do not cut it out; it is the new shoot of a grape tree.
不要剪掉它，那是葡萄樹的新芽。

---

grass
[græs]
名 草

補充 lie down 平躺下來
He lay down on the green grass that he longed for years.
他躺在夢想多年的綠地上。

---

gray
[gre]
形 灰色的 名 灰色

The sky becomes gray because of the dust storm.
天空因沙塵暴而變成一片灰濛濛的樣子。

---

great
[gret]
形 很棒的；大的

I experienced a great change in my second year of graduate school.
研究所第二年，我經歷了很棒的轉變。

greedy
[`gridɪ]
形 貪婪的

補充 arrest 逮捕 / bribe 賄賂
The greedy man was arrested for taking bribes.
那名貪婪的男子因收受賄賂而被逮捕。

green
[grin]
形 綠色的 名 綠色

The real treat in summer is a glass of iced green tea.
夏天最棒的事就是喝杯冰綠茶。

greet
[grit]
動 迎接；問候

The bell rang and Jessie hopped to the door to greet the visitors.
門鈴一響，潔西就跳去門口迎接訪客。

ground
[graʊnd]
名 地面

The cat jumped to the ground to grasp the fast moving toy.
為了抓住快速移動的玩具，貓跳到地上。

group
[grup]
名 一群；團體

Henry gave his opinions on the group project during our discussion.
在討論時，亨利針對團隊企劃提出他的意見。

grow
[gro]
動 成長；種植

補充 三態變化為 grow, grew, grown
My neighbor, Dora, moved to Canada after she grew up.
我鄰居朵拉在長大後就搬到加拿大了。

guard
[gɑrd]
動 保衛 名 警衛

A couple of police officers were guarding the prisoners.
有幾位警察看守著囚犯。

guava
[`gwɑvə]
名 芭樂；番石榴

補充 prefer A to B 喜歡 A 勝過 B
My father prefers guavas to peaches.
和桃子相比，我爸爸更喜歡芭樂。

guess
[gɛs]
動 名 猜想；猜測

Can you guess what will happen next?
你猜得出接下來會發生什麼事嗎？

guest
[gɛst]
名 客人

Lisa directed all the guests to the conference room.
麗莎把客人都帶進了會議室。

guide
[gaɪd]
名 嚮導 **動** 引導

We have arranged a walking tour of the park with the guide.
我們和導遊安排了公園的步行導覽。

guitar
[gɪˋtɑr]
名 吉他

補充 fluency 流暢
To play the guitar with fluency, the rocker practices every day.
為了流暢地演奏吉他，搖滾樂手每天都練習。

gun
[gʌn]
名 槍；砲

補充 suddenly 忽然 / bullet 子彈
Suddenly, a bullet was fired out of a gun.
突然間，子彈從一把槍中射出。

guy
[gaɪ]
名 傢伙；人

I've been seeing a nice-looking guy for months.
我已經跟一位帥哥交往好幾個月了。

gym
[dʒɪm]
名 體育館；健身房

補充 為 gymnasium 的口語說法
A new gym will be constructed in summer and ready in fall.
新的體育館會在夏天興建，秋天竣工。

habit
[`hæbɪt]
名 習慣

Rick has the habit to run 5,000 meters every two days.
瑞克習慣每隔一天就去跑五千公尺。

hair
[hɛr]
名 頭髮

You should dry your hair with a towel after going swimming.
游完泳應該要用毛巾把頭髮擦乾。

haircut
[`hɛr,kʌt]
名 理髮

He woke up and found that his new haircut was done.
他一睡醒，就發現頭髮剪好了。

hairdresser
[`hɛr,drɛsɚ]
名 美髮師

補充 professional 職業的
My cousin is a professional hairdresser.
我堂姊是一名專業美髮師。

half
[hæf]
形 一半的 名 一半

They sold the goods at half price in order to attract more customers.
為了吸引更多顧客，他們以半價銷售商品。

hall
[hɔl]
名 大廳；講堂

補充 convention 會議、大會
The convention was held every year in the county hall since 1992.
一九九二年以後，每年的會議都在郡會堂舉行。

Halloween
[,hælo`in]
名 萬聖節

Stacy is dressed like a Wonder Woman for the Halloween party.
史黛西裝扮成神力女超人，參加萬聖節派對。

ham
[hæm]
名 火腿

He ordered a sandwich with ham and cheese.
他點了一個火腿起司三明治。

hamburger
[`hæmbɝgɚ]
名 漢堡

補充 patty 肉餅
The juicy meat patty is the point to a yummy hamburger.
多汁的肉餅是漢堡的美味關鍵。

hammer
[`hæmɚ]
名 鐵鎚 動 敲打；錘打

My uncle needs a hammer to repair the chair.
我舅舅需要一把鐵鎚來修理這張椅子。

hand
[hænd]
名 手 動 面交；傳遞

補充 hand in sth. 繳交、提交
What are you holding in your hands?
你手裡握著什麼？

handkerchief
[`hæŋkɚˏtʃɪf]
名 手帕

Handkerchief was a common and popular gift in the old days.
手帕在過去是一種常見又受歡迎的禮物。

handle
[`hændl]
動 處理 名 把手

Did your son handle this issue for you?
你兒子替你處理了這個問題嗎？

handsome
[`hænsəm]
形 英俊的

補充 shot 拍攝、電影鏡頭
This is the best shot of the handsome model.
這是那位英俊模特兒的最佳照片。

hang
[hæŋ]
動 把…掛起；吊

補充 當「懸掛」時，三態為 hang, hung, hung
Sam was trying to hang the painting to the wall when I came home.
我回到家時，山姆正試著將畫掛到牆上。

hanger
[`hæŋɚ]
名 衣架；掛鉤

補充 plastic 塑膠製的
The wooden hanger is actually stronger than the plastic one.
木製衣架其實比塑膠製的堅固。

happen
[`hæpən]
動 發生

When the car accident happened, he called the police immediately.
車禍一發生，他立刻打電話給警方。

happy
[`hæpɪ]
形 快樂的

補充 immigrate 從外國移居
Fred is happy to immigrate to Australia.
佛瑞德很高興能移民到澳洲。

hard
[hɑrd]
形 難的；硬的 副 努力地

It is hard to imagine that the low-budget film could win so many awards.
很難想像這部低成本電影能贏得這麼多獎項。

hard-working
[ˌhɑrd`wɝkɪŋ]
形 勤勉的

Ann is the most hard-working employee of the year.
安是整年度最勤勉的員工。

hat
[hæt]
名 帽子

Your new hat goes perfectly with the yellow striped T-shirt.
你的新帽子和那件黃色條紋衫是絕配。

hate
[het]
動 名 憎恨

The history teaches us that war and hate only bring disasters to human.
歷史教導我們，戰爭和憎恨只會為人類帶來災難。

have
[hæv]
動 有 助 已經

補充 stuff 東西、物品
If you have other stuff to do, you can leave.
如果你有別的事情要做，可以離開。

he
[hi]
代 他

補充 him 他（受格）/ his 他的；他的東西
He can be the most gifted teenager for music.
他可能是最具音樂天賦的青少年。

head
[hɛd]
名 頭腦；首領

Please nod your head if you agree with me.
如果你贊同我的意見，請點頭。

headache
[`hɛd‚ek]
名 頭痛

補充 aspirin 阿斯匹靈
Do you have any aspirin for my headache?
你有阿斯匹靈給我止頭痛嗎？

health
[hɛlθ]
名 健康

補充 vitamin 維他命
Vitamins are good for your health.
維他命對你的健康有益。

healthy
[`hɛlθɪ]
形 健康的

My grandmother is in her 90s. She is very healthy for her age.
我祖母九十幾歲，就年齡來看，她很健康。

hear
[hɪr]
動 聽見

補充 sob 啜泣
Did you hear someone sobbing on the balcony?
你剛才有聽見人在陽臺啜泣的聲音嗎？

heart
[hɑrt]
名 心；心臟

補充 disease 疾病
We didn't know Emily has a heart disease.
我們之前不知道艾蜜莉有心臟病。

heat
[hit]
名 熱氣 動 加熱

補充 sunstroke 中暑
Be careful of sunstroke if you stay in the heat for a long time.
如果你長時間待在高溫環境，要小心中暑。

heater
[`hitɚ]
名 暖氣機

Susan left the heater on to keep the house warm.
蘇珊把暖氣開著，以溫暖整棟房子。

heavy
[`hɛvɪ]
形 重的；繁重的

The box is too heavy for Lisa to move on her own.
那個箱子對麗莎而言太重了，她無法獨自搬運。

height
[haɪt]
名 高度；身高

Please tell me your height and weight.
請告訴我你的身高和體重。

helicopter
[`hɛlɪkɑptɚ]
名 直升機

The patient was transported to the hospital by a helicopter.
病人被一架直升機送到醫院。

hello
[hə`lo]
名 哈囉

Ms. Yang gave me a pleasant hello.
楊小姐愉快地向我打招呼。

help
[hɛlp]
動 幫忙

補充 victim 犧牲者、受害者
Many volunteers went to the country to help the victims.
許多義工前往該國救助災民。

helpful
[`hɛlpfəl]
形 有幫助的；有用的

He made several helpful suggestions at the meeting.
他在會議上提了幾個有用的建議。

hen
[hɛn]
名 母雞

補充 hatch 孵出
The hen had hatched many eggs until it died.
這隻母雞孵育了非常多蛋，直至死亡。

here
[hɪr]
副 在這裡

The man helped us move the table here.
男子幫忙我們把桌子移到這裡。

hero
[`hɪro]
名 英雄

補充 fairy 幻想中的 / tale 故事
A hero always wins at the end of a fairy tale.
在童話故事的最後，英雄總會獲勝。

herself
[hɚ`sɛlf]
代 她自己（反身代名詞）

補充 反身代名詞必須與主詞吻合
Lisa dressed herself up for the ceremony.
麗莎盛裝赴會。

hide
[haɪd]
動 躲；隱藏

補充 dig 挖洞、挖溝（過去式 dug）
The dog dug a hole to hide its bone.
這隻狗挖洞來藏骨頭。

high
[haɪ]
形 高的 副 向高處

I can't believe he bought that vase at such a high price.
不敢相信他竟用這麼高的價格買那個花瓶。

highway
[`haɪˌwe]
名 高速公路；幹道

The highway was closed because of the coming storm.
因為即將來臨的暴風雪，那條高速公路被關閉。

hike
[haɪk]
動 健行 名 遠足

Adam hiked for 5 hours without seeing anyone in the mountains.
在山區走了五小時，亞當沒遇見半個人。

hill
[hɪl]
名 丘陵；小山

補充 cottage 小屋、農舍
My grandfather has a small cottage on the hill.
我祖父在山丘上有間小農舍。

himself
[hɪm`sɛlf]
代 他自己（反身代名詞）

補充 boast 吹噓、自吹自擂
Henry always likes to boast himself.
亨利總是喜歡吹捧自己。

hip
[hɪp]
名 臀部

The guy put his hands on his hips and shrugged his shoulders.
小伙子將雙手放在臀部並聳了聳肩。

hippo
[`hɪpo]
名 河馬

補充 完整英文為 hippopotamus
Mandy drew a hippo on the cover of her textbook.
曼蒂在她課本的封面上畫了一隻河馬。

hire
[haɪr]
動 僱用

Robert hires someone to do it.
羅伯特僱用了某人去做這件事。

history
[`hɪstərɪ]
名 歷史

補充 assign 指派、指定
Our history teacher assigned us lots of summer homework.
歷史老師派給我們很多暑假作業。

hit
[hɪt]
動 名 打擊

補充 三態變化為 hit, hit, hit
The volleyball hit me when I was talking to our coach.
在與教練談話時，那顆排球打中了我。

hobby
[`hɑbɪ]
名 嗜好

My hobbies are reading and listening to music.
我的嗜好是閱讀與聽音樂。

hold
[hold]
動 拿著；舉行

補充 三態變化為 hold, held, held
The two men held hands and signed the contract.
那兩位男士握手，簽下合約。

hole
[hol]
名 洞

Andy was surprised to discover a hole on the wall.
安迪驚訝地發現牆上有個洞。

holiday
[`hɑlə‚de]
名 假日

We are going to Sweden for our holidays.
我們假期時會去瑞典。

home
[hom]
名 家 副 在家

The typhoon is coming. Please go back home now.
颱風快來了，現在請立刻回家。

homesick
[`hom‚sɪk]
形 想家的

She had strong homesick when she first moved to Paris.
她剛搬到巴黎時，非常想家。

homework
[`hom‚wɝk]
名 家庭作業

Michael finished his homework and put it into the drawer.
麥可寫完作業，並將它放進了抽屜。

honest
[`ɑnɪst]
形 誠實的

As your friend, I need you to be honest to me.
作為你的朋友，我需要你對我坦誠以對。

honesty
[`ɑnɪstɪ]
名 誠實

補充 virtue 美德、德行
He said the greatest virtue in a man is honesty.
他表示一個人最大的美德就是誠實。

honey
[`hʌnɪ]
名 蜂蜜；心愛的人

補充 tub 桶、木盆
The woman bought tubs of honey from the beekeeper.
女人向養蜂人買了好幾桶蜂蜜。

hop
[hɑp]
動 單腳跳;快速跳上(車輛)

The teacher made Tom hop around the track for his lateness.
因為遲到,老師叫湯姆單腳跳繞操場。

hope
[hop]
動 **名** 希望

I hope I can pass all my courses this semester.
我希望我這學期的所有課程都能及格。

horrible
[`hɔrəbḷ]
形 可怕的

Your room is in a horrible mess. Can you tidy it up?
你的房間真的是一團糟,你可以收拾一下嗎?

horse
[hɔrs]
名 馬

The horse racing is not popular in Taiwan.
在臺灣,賽馬並不風行。

hospital
[`hɑspɪtḷ]
名 醫院

The doctor said you must stay at the hospital tonight.
醫生說你今晚必須留在醫院。

host
[host]
名 主人;主持人 **動** 主辦

補充 champagne 香檳
The host toasted his guests with champagne.
主人舉起香檳,向所有賓客敬酒。

hot
[hɑt]
形 熱的

補充 icy 多冰的、冰冷的
Do you want your tea hot or icy?
你想喝熱茶還是冰茶?

hot dog
片 熱狗

補充 badly 嚴重地、厲害地
Polly wants to eat hot dogs in that shop badly.
波莉非常想要吃那家店賣的熱狗。

hotel
[ho`tɛl]
名 旅館

The hotel we're staying at provides dinner and breakfast.
我們住宿的旅館提供晚餐及早餐。

hour
[auɚ]
名 小時

Albert swims for one hour every morning before class.
每天上午的課程前，亞伯特會游泳一小時。

house
[haʊs]
名 房子

We are having a party at my house. Do you want to join us?
我們要在我家舉辦派對，你要參加嗎？

housewife
[`haʊs,waɪf]
名 家庭主婦

My daughter-in-law is a housewife.
我媳婦是一位家庭主婦。

housework
[`haʊs,wɜk]
名 家事

The musician hired an assistant to do housework.
那位音樂家僱用了一位助理來做家事。

how
[haʊ]
副 如何

How much is the ticket of the concert?
這場音樂會的門票多少錢呢？

however
[haʊ`ɛvɚ]
連 然而 副 無論如何

Tim always stays up late; however, he gets up early every morning.
提姆總是熬夜到很晚，然而，他每天都很早起床。

hug
[hʌg]
動 名 擁抱

補充 動詞 + with joy 表示「開心地做某事」
The little girl hugs her cat with joy.
小女孩開心地抱住她的貓。

human
[`hjumən]
形 人類的　名 人；人類

補充 nowadays 現今 / human being 人類
Nowadays, human beings depend on technology a lot.
現今，人類非常依賴科技。

humble
[`hʌmbļ]
形 謙恭的

Although he is the president, he is very humble to everyone.
雖然身為總統，但他對每個人都很謙恭有禮。

humid
[`hjumɪd]
形 潮溼的

補充 worse 為 bad（形容詞）的比較級
The humid weather made the summer night even worse.
夏天夜晚的溼氣讓人更加難受。

humor
[`hjuməʳ]
名 幽默

補充 sense of humor 幽默感
The actor showed his sense of humor in the interview.
那名演員在訪問過程中展現了他的幽默感。

humorous
[`hjumərəs]
形 幽默的

A humorous scene added interest to that movie.
幽默的一幕為那部電影增添了趣味。

hundred
[`hʌndrəd]
形 一百的　名 一百

The five-year-old boy can count to one hundred.
這個五歲的小男孩會從一數到一百。

hunger
[`hʌngəʳ]
名 飢餓；饑荒

補充 donate 捐獻、捐贈
Donating a little money could save the children from hunger.
捐一點錢就能拯救那些孩童免於飢餓。

hungry
[`hʌngrɪ]
形 飢餓的

補充 eat up 吃光、用完
Leo was so hungry that he ate up the sandwich within seconds.
里歐非常餓，在幾秒內就把三明治吃掉了。

hunt
[hʌnt]
動 打獵；獵取

The man packed his bow and arrows to hunt for food.
為了食物，男人備好打獵用的弓箭。

hunter
[`hʌntə]
名 獵人

補充 pull the trigger 扣扳機
The hunter aimed at the rabbit and pulled his trigger.
獵人瞄準兔子並扣下扳機。

hurry
[`hɜrɪ]
名 匆忙 動 趕快

He left the restaurant in such a hurry that he forgot to tip.
他離開餐廳時太匆忙，忘了給小費。

hurt
[hɜt]
動 傷害；使疼痛

補充 twist 扭曲
I didn't mean to hurt him, so don't twist my words.
我沒有想要傷害他，別曲解我的話。

husband
[`hʌzbənd]
名 丈夫

This novel describes all kinds of problems between husband and wife.
這本小說描述了夫妻之間的各種問題。

Unit
09 Ii 字頭單字

MP3 09

I
[aɪ]
代 我（第一人稱單數主格）

補充 me 我（受格）/ my 我的 / mine 我的東西
I want to be a scientist since I was a child.
我從小就希望成為一名科學家。

ice
[aɪs]
名 冰

補充 bruise 瘀青、青腫
Use some ice to treat the bruise, or it will get worse.
用冰敷一下瘀青，不然會惡化。

ice cream
片 冰淇淋

Ice cream is the most popular snack among children.
冰淇淋是最受孩子們歡迎的點心。

idea
[aɪˋdɪə]
名 主意

補充 fantasy 幻想 / fiction 小說
The idea of writing a fantasy fiction started several years ago.
幾年前開始就有了寫奇幻小說的想法。

if
[ɪf]
連 如果；是否

If I were a millionaire, I would donate more money to people in need.
如果我是百萬富翁，就會捐更多錢給窮困的人。

ignore
[ɪgˋnor]
動 不理睬

We shouldn't ignore the problems caused by climate change.
我們不該忽視氣候變遷所造成的問題。

ill
[ɪl]
形 生病的 名 不幸

Ann didn't come to class today because she is terribly ill.
安病得很重，所以今天沒來上課。

imagine
[ɪˋmædʒɪn]
動 想像

補充 get married 結婚（為慣用語）
I can't imagine that Daniel is getting married.
我不敢相信丹尼爾要結婚了。

impolite
[ˌɪmpəˋlaɪt]
形 沒禮貌的

It is impolite to judge people by their appearance.
以貌取人是很無禮的。

importance
[ɪmˈpɔrtn̩s]
名 重要性

The manager emphasized the importance of teamwork in today's meeting.
經理在今天的會議中強調了團隊合作的重要性。

important
[ɪmˈpɔrtn̩t]
形 重要的

My parents are the most important family of mine.
父母是我最重要的親人。

impossible
[ɪmˈpɑsəbl̩]
形 不可能的

補充 undo 消除 / injury 傷害
It's impossible to undo the injury of her heart.
她心中的傷痕不可能消除得了。

improve
[ɪmˈpruv]
動 改善

補充 last century 上個世紀
The study of diseases improved a lot in the last century.
這一世紀以來，對疾病的研究大有進展。

in
[ɪn]
介 在⋯裡面

補充 horror 恐怖 / by chance 偶然
Christine got her leading role in the horror movie by chance.
克莉絲汀偶然地成為這部恐怖片的主演。

inch
[ɪntʃ]
名 英寸

We need a table about 70 inches in width to fit in that corner.
我們需要一張約七十英寸寬的桌子，擺在那個角落。

include
[ɪnˈklud]
動 包含

There are four people in my family, including me.
包含我的話，我家總共有四個人。

income
[ˈɪnkʌm]
名 收入

補充 double 當動詞時表「使加倍」
He doubled his income by taking two part-time jobs.
他打了兩份工讓收入倍增。

increase
[ɪnˋkris]
動 名 增加

當名詞時，重音會放在第一音節
The runner increased the distance and speed.
跑者增加了距離，並提升速度。

independent
[ˏɪndɪˋpɛndənt]
形 獨立的

Argentina became independent from Spain in 1816.
阿根廷在西元一八一六年脫離西班牙獨立。

indicate
[ˋɪndəˏket]
動 指出

tone 語氣、腔調
Her tone indicated that she didn't believe what we said.
她的語調表明她不相信我們所說的話。

influence
[ˋɪnfluəns]
名 影響

have an influence on sb. 對某人有影響
My mother had a great influence on me.
母親對我的影響很大。

information
[ˏɪnfəˋmeʃən]
名 資訊

You may find the information in the reference section of the library.
你可以在圖書館的參考書區找到資訊。

ink
[ɪŋk]
名 墨水

run out of 用完、耗盡
This printer is running out of ink.
這台印表機沒有墨水了。

insect
[ˋɪnsɛkt]
名 昆蟲

Most insects have six legs and wings.
大多數昆蟲有六隻腳和翅膀。

inside
[ɪnˋsaɪd]
介 在…裡面 **副** 在裡面

Make sure that everything you need is inside the box.
要確保你所需的一切都在箱子裡面。

insist
[ɪn`sɪst]
動 堅持

He **insists** on living meaningfully even though he only has 2 years to live.
即使只剩兩年壽命，他也堅持要活得有意義。

inspire
[ɪn`spaɪr]
動 鼓舞；啟發

補充 set up 建立 / graduation 畢業
My sister **inspires** me to set up a company after graduation.
我姐姐激勵我畢業後成立一間公司。

instant
[`ɪnstənt]
形 即時的 **名** 瞬間

I need a cup of **instant** coffee every morning to wake up.
我每天早上要喝一杯即溶咖啡才能醒過來。

instrument
[`ɪnstrəmənt]
名 儀器

Which **instrument** are you playing for the concert tonight?
今晚的演奏會你將演奏哪一種樂器？

intelligent
[ɪn`tɛlədʒnt]
形 有才智的

Ivy is an **intelligent** woman. She never fights against John in public.
艾薇是個聰明的女人，她絕不在公開場合跟約翰吵架。

interest
[`ɪntərɪst]
名 興趣；利益 **動** 使有興趣

Wendy has shown **interest** in music and singing since childhood.
溫蒂從小就展現出對音樂與歌唱的興趣。

interested
[`ɪntərɪstɪd]
形 感興趣的

補充 be interested in 對…有興趣
Jerry has been **interested** in performing in front of people.
傑瑞一直以來都喜歡在眾人面前表演。

interesting
[`ɪntərɪstɪŋ]
形 有趣的

Mr. Lee is nice and teaches us in an **interesting** way.
李老師人很好，教學方式也很有趣。

international
[ˌɪntə·ˈnæʃənḷ]
形 國際的

I share an apartment with other international students.
我與其他國際學生合租一間公寓。

Internet
[ˈɪntə·ˌnɛt]
名 網際網路

補充 invention 發明物
The Internet is the greatest invention in 20th century.
網際網路被認為是二十世紀最偉大的發明。

interrupt
[ˌɪntə·ˈrʌpt]
動 打斷（談話、工作等）

Please don't interrupt her while she is writing.
請不要在她寫作時打擾她。

interview
[ˈɪntə·ˌvju]
動 名 面談；採訪

補充 committee 委員會 / whole 整個的
The parent committee interviewed her for the whole morning.
家長委員會和她面談了一整個早上。

into
[ˈɪntu]
介 到…裡面；進入

Jerry just moved into a new house last week.
傑瑞上週才搬進新家。

introduce
[ˌɪntrə·ˈdjus]
動 介紹

James introduced his new girlfriend to us.
詹姆士介紹他的新女友給我們認識。

invent
[ɪnˈvɛnt]
動 發明

Thomas Edison invented the first phonograph in 1877.
湯瑪士‧愛迪生在一八七七年發明了第一臺留聲機。

invitation
[ˌɪnvə·ˈteʃən]
名 邀請

Rita sent her wedding invitations to her close friends.
芮塔把她的結婚請帖寄給好友們。

invite
[ɪn`vaɪt]
動 邀請

Jenny invited us to her new house. I can't wait!
珍妮邀請我們去她的新家，我等不及了！

iron
[`aɪən]
名 鐵；熨斗 **動** 熨燙

補充 foundation 基礎 / industrial 工業的
Iron and steel are the foundation of an industrial country.
鋼鐵是工業國家的根本。

island
[`aɪlənd]
名 島嶼

補充 hover（直升機）停留在空中
The helicopter hovered over the island for a while.
直升機在島嶼上空盤旋了一會兒。

it
[ɪt]
代 它；這；那

補充 its 它的 / itself 它自己
She started to clean the room to make it tidy.
她開始打掃房間，以保持整潔。

item
[`aɪtəm]
名 項目

Don't you think that all the items I bought are good?
你不覺得我買的東西都很好嗎？

Unit 10 Jj 字頭單字

MP3 10

jacket
[`dʒækɪt]
名 夾克；外套

My brother told me not to wear his jacket.
我哥哥叫我不要穿他的夾克。

jam
[dʒæm]
名 果醬;堵塞 動 不能動彈

My daughter is not a big fan of jam.
我女兒不愛吃果醬。

January
[`dʒænju,ɛrɪ]
名 一月

補充 schedule 安排 / release 發行
The movie is scheduled for release in January.
這部電影預定一月發行。

jazz
[dʒæz]
名 爵士樂

My friend invited me to go to a jazz concert.
朋友邀請我去參加一場爵士演奏會。

jealous
[`dʒɛləs]
形 嫉妒的

John is so jealous that he couldn't allow his wife talking to other men.
約翰因嫉妒而不准太太和別的男人說話。

jeans
[dʒinz]
名 牛仔褲

The model looks really good in white T-shirt and jeans.
那名模特兒穿白 T 恤和牛仔褲真的很好看。

jeep
[dʒip]
名 吉普車

Have you ever driven a jeep? It must be exciting.
你開過吉普車嗎?感覺一定很刺激。

job
[dʒɑb]
名 職業;工作

He needs to do a part-time job to support his family.
為了維持家裡的生計,他必須兼差。

jog
[dʒɑg]
動 慢跑

Mr. Anderson jogs every night before bed.
安德森先生每天晚上睡前都會去慢跑。

join
[dʒɔɪn]
動 加入；參加

Jimmy joined the soccer team when he was in senior high school.
吉米高中時期參加了足球隊。

joke
[dʒok]
名 笑話 **動** 開玩笑

Larry spent the evening telling jokes and funny stories.
賴瑞整個晚上都在說笑話和有趣的故事。

journalist
[`dʒɜnḷɪst]
名 記者

She used to be a journalist and now is an author.
她以前是記者，現在則是一名作家。

joy
[dʒɔɪ]
名 喜悅；樂趣

補充 burst 爆發 / proposal 求婚
He was bursting with joy when his girlfriend accepted his proposal.
女友接受他的求婚時，他高興極了。

judge
[dʒʌdʒ]
動 判斷；審判 **名** 法官

Do you know who is going to judge my case?
你知道誰會負責審判我的案子嗎？

juice
[dʒus]
名 果汁

補充 bartender 酒保
The bartender mixed juice with whiskey.
這名酒保把果汁和威士忌混合在一起。

July
[dʒu`laɪ]
名 七月

I hope to find our perfect home by July.
我希望在七月之前找到我們理想的家。

jump
[dʒʌmp]
動 跳躍

補充 excitement 興奮、激動
The children were jumping up and down with excitement.
孩子們興奮地跳上跳下。

June
[dʒun]
名 六月

補充 unemployment 失業 / rate 比率
The unemployment rate reached a new high in June.
六月的失業率創下新高。

junior high school
片 初級中學；國中

Linda's daughter is about to go to junior high school.
琳達的女兒要上國中了。

just
[dʒʌst]
副 正好；剛才

補充 cost a fortune 花一大筆錢
It's just popcorn; it won't cost you a fortune.
這只是爆米花而已，不會花掉你多少錢的。

Kk 字頭單字

MP3 11

kangaroo
[ˌkæŋɡəˋru]
名 袋鼠

We saw many kangaroos when we were in Australia.
我們在澳洲時看到很多袋鼠。

keep
[kip]
動 保留；保持

補充 keep one's promise 某人遵守諾言
He always keeps his promise.
他總是信守承諾。

ketchup
[ˋkɛtʃəp]
名 番茄醬

補充 grocery store 雜貨店
Can you get me a bottle of ketchup from the grocery store?
你可以幫我到雜貨店買一瓶番茄醬嗎？

key
[ki]
名 鑰匙

Tommy took a large ring of keys from his backpack.
湯米從他的背包裡拿出一大串鑰匙。

kick
[kɪk]
動 名 踢

Jackson kicked the ball towards the goal.
傑克森把球踢向球門。

kid
[kɪd]
名 小孩 動 戲弄

The teacher punished the kid who broke the window.
老師處罰了打破窗戶的那個孩子。

kill
[kɪl]
動 殺

補充 civilian 市民、平民
The bomber had killed eight civilians last night.
炸彈客昨晚殺害了八位市民。

kilogram
[`kɪlə,græm]
名 公斤

補充 使用時經常縮寫為 kg
The blue fin tuna caught today weighs over three hundred kilograms.
今天捕獲的黑鮪魚重量超過三百公斤。

kilometer
[kɪ`lɑmətə]
名 公里

補充 使用時經常縮寫為 km
The bus was traveled under sixty kilometers per hour.
那台公車每小時的時速不到六十公里。

kind
[kaɪnd]
形 仁慈的 名 種類

補充 all kinds of 各種的、許多不同的
We all like Paula because she is a kind girl.
寶拉是一位仁慈的女孩，我們都很喜歡她。

kindergarten
[`kɪndə,gɑrtn]
名 幼稚園

Our twins are in kindergarten now.
我們的雙胞胎現在唸幼稚園。

king
[kɪŋ]
名 國王

Henry II became King of England in 1154.
亨利二世在西元一一五四年成為英格蘭國王。

kingdom
[`kɪŋdəm]
名 王國

補充 legendary 傳說的 / bury 埋葬
The legendary kingdom was buried under the desert.
這個傳說中的王國被埋在這片沙漠底下。

kiss
[kɪs]
名 吻 動 親吻

Abby's parents always give her a kiss before she goes to bed.
艾比的父母總會在她睡覺前給她一個吻。

kitchen
[`kɪtʃɪn]
名 廚房

My mother is making dinner for us in the kitchen.
媽媽正在廚房為我們做晚餐。

kite
[kaɪt]
名 風箏

補充 fly a kite 放風箏
It was a lovely summer afternoon to fly a kite in the park.
那是一個適合去公園放風箏的宜人夏日午後。

kitten
[`kɪtn̩]
名 小貓

補充 adorable 可愛的（口語用法）
The newborn kitten keeps meowing, which looks very adorable.
剛出生的小貓一直喵喵叫，看起來很可愛。

knee
[ni]
名 膝蓋

Sandra will have an operation on her knee next week.
珊卓拉下星期要動膝蓋手術。

knife
[naɪf]
名 刀子

補充 core 果核
She removed the core of the fruit with a knife carefully.
她小心地用刀去除水果的果核。

knock
[nɑk]
名 動 敲

The three-times knock was a sign of his brother's coming.
敲三聲是用來表示他哥哥來了的暗號。

know
[no]
動 知道

補充 in private 私下地 / in public 公開地
I don't know why he wants to meet me in private.
我不知道他為何要私下見我。

knowledge
[`nɑlɪdʒ]
名 學問；知識

補充 chimpanzee 黑猩猩 / fascinate 迷住
Jane Goodall's knowledge on chimpanzees fascinates me.
珍古德對於黑猩猩的知識令我著迷不已。

koala
[ko`ɑlə]
名 無尾熊

Do you know how a female koala carries her baby?
你知道雌性無尾熊是如何攜帶小孩的嗎？

Unit 12 LI 字頭單字

MP3 12

lack
[læk]
動 名 缺乏

補充 動詞 lack 後面直接加缺乏的東西
My brother lacks confidence and courage.
我哥哥缺乏自信與勇氣。

lady
[`ledɪ]
名 女士；淑女

補充 attract 吸引
Gloria is a fair lady who always attracts people's attention.
葛洛莉亞是位優雅的淑女，總會吸引眾人目光。

lake
[lek]
名 湖；湖泊

The boy scouts will camp by the lake this weekend.
這群童子軍這個週末將在湖邊露營。

lamb
[læm]
名 小羊；羊肉

補充 chop（豬、羊的）肋排
The restaurant is famous for roast lamb chop.
這家餐廳以烤羊排聞名。

lamp
[læmp]
名 燈

補充 bedside 床旁的
Lisa read by the light of the bedside lamp.
麗莎藉著床頭燈的光線閱讀。

land
[lænd]
名 陸地 **動** 登陸

補充 percent 百分比 / surface 表面
About thirty percent of the earth's surface is covered by land.
地球表面大約百分之三十被陸地覆蓋。

language
[`læŋgwɪdʒ]
名 語言

補充 other than 除了
What language do you speak other than Chinese?
除了中文，你還會講什麼語言？

lantern
[`læntən]
名 燈籠

The Taiwan Lantern Festival is an annual event.
臺灣燈會是一個年度活動。

large
[lɑrdʒ]
形 大的

補充 multinational 跨國的
It is a large multinational company with many branches.
那是一間大型跨國企業，有很多分公司。

last
[læst]
形 最後的 **動** 持續

I saw him chatting with the victim last night.
我看到他昨晚與受害人聊天。

late
[let]
形 晚的；遲的

補充 be supposed to 應該 / attend 參加
You are not supposed to be late when you attend an interview.
當你參加面試的時候不應該遲到。

latter
[`lætɚ]
形 後者的

In the latter part of the book, one of the characters became mad.
在書的後半部，其中一位角色瘋了。

laugh
[læf]
動 笑 名 笑聲

He kept laughing while watching the hilarious comedy.
他觀賞令人捧腹的喜劇片，一直大笑。

law
[lɔ]
名 法律

補充 application 申請書
Susan's application for Harvard Law School is rejected.
蘇珊的哈佛法學院申請書被駁回。

lawyer
[`lɔjɚ]
名 律師

補充 evidence 證據
The lawyer handed the evidence to the police.
律師把證物交給警方。

lay
[le]
動 產卵；放置

補充 三態變化為 lay, laid, laid
My robin has laid two eggs.
我的知更鳥已生了兩顆蛋。

lazy
[`lezɪ]
形 懶惰的

The nanny was mean and lazy, so no children liked her.
那名保姆既刻薄又懶惰，沒有小孩喜歡她。

lead
[lid]
動 引導；帶領

補充 三態變化為 lead, led, led
I wonder what led him to quit smoking.
我很好奇是什麼事導致他戒菸？

leader
[`lidə]
名 領袖

Tim is a great leader and nobody dislikes him in the office.
提姆是名成功的領導者，公司裡沒有人不喜歡他。

leaf
[lif]
名 樹葉

補充 leaves 為複數形
There are many dead leaves under the tree.
這棵樹下有很多枯葉。

learn
[lɜn]
動 學習

I went to the driving school to learn how to drive a car.
我去駕訓班上課，學習如何開車。

least
[list]
名 最少；至少 副 最少

補充 at least 至少
It took me at least five hours to drive from Taipei to Kaohsiung.
從臺北開車到高雄至少要花我五個鐘頭。

leave
[liv]
動 離開；丟下 名 休假

補充 動詞三態變化為 leave, left, left
It's hard for her to leave her sick husband and go on business.
她很難離開生病的丈夫去出差。

left
[lɛft]
形 左邊的 副 向左

補充 cupboard 碗櫃、櫥櫃
To the left of the cupboard, you will find an iron box.
在碗櫃的左邊，你會找到一個鐵盒子。

leg
[lɛg]
名 腿

The fall from the tree broke his right leg.
他從樹上跌下來，摔斷了右腿。

lemon
[`lɛmən]
名 檸檬

The bakery is known for its lemon pie.
這家麵包店以檸檬派聞名。

lend
[lɛnd]
動 出借

補充 三態變化為 lend, lent, lent
Can you lend me your laptop tomorrow?
你明天能不能借我筆電？

less
[lɛs]
形 較少的

Joe has very less money, so he cannot go traveling with us.
喬沒什麼錢，所以他無法和我們去旅遊。

lesson
[`lɛsn̩]
名 課；教訓

補充 learn a lesson 學到教訓
I decided to take the photography lessons.
我決定去上攝影課。

let
[lɛt]
動 讓

補充 三態變化為 let, let, let
Henry's mother doesn't let him eat the cake.
亨利的媽媽不讓他吃蛋糕。

letter
[`lɛtɚ]
名 信；字母

補充 delivery 投遞、傳送
I sent the letter by express delivery; you shall get it by tomorrow.
我以快遞寄出信件，你明天應該就能收到了。

lettuce
[`lɛtɪs]
名 生菜；萵苣

Lettuce is commonly used in cooking.
萵苣被普遍使用於烹飪中。

level
[`lɛvl̩]
名 程度 形 水平的

The students have reached the advanced level already.
那群學生已達高級班的水準了。

library
[`laɪ͵brɛrɪ]
名 圖書館

I will go to the library to check the reference books on the list.
我會去圖書館查清單上的參考文獻。

lick
[lɪk]
動 舔

My dog likes to lick my face.
我的狗喜歡舔我的臉。

lid
[lɪd]
名 蓋子

Paul forgot to put the lid on the pot last night.
保羅昨晚忘記把蓋子蓋回鍋子上。

lie
[laɪ]
動 說謊；躺 **名** 謊言

補充 「說謊」的三態變化為 lie, lied, lied
She lied about her family's situation to her friends.
她對朋友說謊，隱瞞了家裡的情況。

life
[laɪf]
名 人生；生命

The brave man saved the president's life.
這名勇敢的男子救了總統的命。

lift
[lɪft]
動 **名** 舉起

They helped the man lift the heavy desk.
他們幫忙那位男士抬起沉重的桌子。

light
[laɪt]
名 光線；燈
形 輕的；明亮的

A sudden light made me feel uncomfortable.
突如其來的亮光令我感到不適。

lightning
[`laɪtnɪŋ]
名 閃電

There was a sudden lightning striking in the sky.
突然有道閃電劃破天際。

like
[laɪk]
動 喜歡 **介** 像；如

The girl likes her mother's bedtime stories very much.
那名女孩非常喜歡母親講的睡前故事。

likely
[`laɪklɪ]
形 很可能的

He's more likely to join the dance club instead of debate club.
他很可能參加熱舞社，而非辯論社。

limit
[`lɪmɪt]
名 動 限制

補充 challenge 挑戰 / physical 身體的
The race challenged the physical limits of the players.
那場比賽挑戰參賽者的體能極限。

line
[laɪn]
名 線條；隊伍 動 排隊

The students formed a line in front of the classroom.
學生在教室前排成一列。

link
[lɪŋk]
名 環節；聯繫 動 連接

補充 establish 建立
They hope to establish a link between the two companies.
他們希望建立起兩家公司的聯繫。

lion
[`laɪən]
名 獅子

Have you ever seen the movie *The Lion King*?
你看過《獅子王》這部電影嗎？

lip
[lɪp]
名 嘴脣

I cannot stand a dog licking my lips.
我無法忍受狗舔我的嘴脣。

liquid
[`lɪkwɪd]
名 液體

The kids used liquid soap to wash their hands.
孩子們用洗手乳洗手。

list
[lɪst]
名 清單；列表
動 把…編列成表

There are a lot of things on my shopping list.
我的購物清單上有很多東西。

listen
[ˋlɪsn̩]
動 傾聽

I used to listen to pop music, but I love jazz more now.
我以前都聽流行歌曲，但現在更喜歡爵士樂。

liter
[ˋlitɚ]
名 公升

We need a liter of cream to make the cake.
我們需要一公升奶油來做這個蛋糕。

little
[ˋlɪtl̩]
形 小的；很少的 **副** 一點點

I've been learning dancing since I was a little girl.
我從小就開始學習舞蹈。

live
[lɪv]
動 居住；生存

I've never been to Switzerland, but my sister lives there.
我從來沒去過瑞士，但我姐姐住在那裡。

living room
片 客廳

Ms. Smith decorated the living room with bright colored curtains.
史密斯小姐用亮色的窗簾裝飾客廳。

loaf
[lof]
名 一條（麵包）

I want a loaf of bread to go.
我要外帶一條麵包。

local
[ˋlokl̩]
形 本地的 **名** 當地居民

His work attracted our attention after being reported by the local media.
他的作品被當地媒體報導後，引起我們的注意。

lock
[lɑk]
動 鎖住 **名** 鎖

Jimmy forgot to lock the front door when he left home this morning.
吉米今天早上出門時忘記將前門上鎖。

locker
[`lɑkɚ]
名 置物櫃

補充 通常指公眾場所的公用置物櫃
The man took out a pair of sneakers from his locker.
男子從置物櫃裡拿出一雙運動鞋。

lonely
[`lonlɪ]
形 孤單的；寂寞的

Emma feels lonely because her roommate is out.
艾瑪覺得很孤單，因為她的室友出門了。

long
[lɔŋ]
形 長的；長時間的

補充 conclusion 結論
The long meeting did not come to a conclusion.
那個冗長的會議並沒有討論出個結果。

look
[lʊk]
動 看 名 看；表情

補充 look for 尋找
The sales number does not look good over the past three months.
過去三個月來的銷售數字不佳。

lose
[luz]
動 輸；失去

補充 三態變化為 lose, lost, lost
The man has lost two houses for gambling.
因為賭博，男子已經輸掉了兩棟房子。

loser
[`luzɚ]
名 輸家；失敗者

Cheer up! Don't make yourself look like a total loser.
振作點！不要讓自己看起來像個失敗者。

lot
[lɑt]
名 很多；一塊土地

I am afraid that we might face a lot of trouble with the project.
我擔心這個計畫可能會面臨許多困難。

loud
[laʊd]
形 大聲的

The loud noise stopped everyone from having lunch.
噪音太大聲，吵得大家用不了午餐。

love
[lʌv]
動 愛；喜歡 名 愛

Ivy loves all kinds of sports, especially swimming.
艾薇喜歡所有類型的運動，尤其是游泳。

lovely
[`lʌvlɪ]
形 可愛的；動人的

Dora is a lovely girl who carries a big smile every day.
朵拉是位可愛的女孩，每天都帶著大大的笑容。

low
[lo]
形 低的；矮的

The birth rate is still low this year.
今年的出生率仍然很低。

lucky
[`lʌkɪ]
形 幸運的

Actually, it was just a lucky guess.
事實上，那只是碰巧猜中而已。

lunch
[lʌntʃ]
名 午餐

I usually have lunch in school's cafeteria.
我通常會在學校的自助餐廳裡吃午餐。

Unit 13 Mm 字頭單字

MP3 13

ma'am
[mæm]
名 女士

補充 madam 的口語用法
Ma'am, may I take your luggage to the guest room?
女士，我可以幫您將行李提進客房嗎？

machine
[məˋʃin]
名 機器

補充 solar 太陽的、日光的
This new machine is driven by solar energy.
這台新型機器是用太陽能來驅動的。

mad
[mæd]
形 發火的;發狂的

The professor got mad because he didn't show up on time.
他沒有準時出席,教授氣得臉色發青。

magazine
[ˏmæɡəˋzin]
名 雜誌

補充 flip through 快速翻閱
Dr. Yang flipped through the magazine to find a report.
楊醫師快速翻閱雜誌,尋找一篇報導。

magic
[ˋmædʒɪk]
名 魔術 形 魔術的

補充 audience 觀眾 / entertain 使娛樂
The audience was entertained by his magic.
他的魔術娛樂了觀眾。

magician
[məˋdʒɪʃən]
名 魔術師

All the tricks the magician had practiced were marvelous.
魔術師所變的戲法非常不可思議。

mail
[mel]
動 寄信 名 信件

He asked the secretary to forward the mail for him.
他請祕書替他轉交這封信。

mailman
[ˋmelˏmæn]
名 郵差

The mailman brought us a large package.
郵差給我們送來一個大包裹。

main
[men]
形 主要的

補充 entire 整個的
The main steel bars carry the entire weight of the building.
主要的鋼筋支撐著整棟建築物的重量。

major
[`medʒɚ]
形 主要的　名 主修科目

補充 route 路線、路程
It was a major route for trade in the 18th century.
那是十八世紀的主要貿易路線。

make
[mek]
動 製造；使得

補充 driveway 私人車道
Every Christmas, we would make a snowman beside the driveway.
每年聖誕節，我們都會在車道旁做一個雪人。

male
[mel]
名 男性　形 男性的

Their target customer is young males, from 18 to 28.
他們的目標客戶為十八歲至二十八歲的年輕男性。

mall
[mɔl]
名 購物中心

Do you want to go shopping at the mall with us?
你想跟我們去購物中心買東西嗎？

man
[mæn]
名 男人；人類

The man is so humorous that many girls like him.
這名男子非常幽默，所以很多女孩喜歡他。

manager
[`mænɪdʒɚ]
名 經理

補充 promote 晉升
Mike has been promoted to general manager yesterday.
麥克昨天被拔擢為總經理。

mango
[`mæŋgo]
名 芒果

We pick mangoes in Uncle John's yard every summer.
我們每年夏天會到約翰叔叔的庭院摘芒果。

manner
[`mænɚ]
名 舉止；態度

補充 a lack of sth. 缺少某物
His manner suggested a lack of interest in that movie.
從他的態度可看出他對那部電影不感興趣。

many
[`mɛnɪ]
形 很多的 **代** 許多

This book has many pictures to show you how to cook.
這本書裡有許多照片，教你如何烹飪。

map
[mæp]
名 地圖

According to the map, the restaurant should be at the corner.
根據地圖指示，餐廳應該就在轉角處。

March
[mɑrtʃ]
名 三月

補充 小寫 march 表「行軍」的意思
She expects me to report for work on March the fifth.
她預期我於三月五日報到上班。

mark
[mɑrk]
名 記號 **動** 做記號

Do you see the mark on the wall?
你有看到牆上的記號嗎？

marker
[`mɑrkɚ]
名 標誌；馬克筆

The student took out her marker pen and drew a line.
那名學生拿出馬克筆，畫了一條線。

market
[`mɑrkɪt]
名 市場

There's a small market near my house.
我家附近有一間小型超市。

married
[`mærɪd]
形 已婚的

My grandfather has been married with my grandmother for 50 years.
我祖父跟祖母結婚已有五十年了。

marry
[`mærɪ]
動 結婚

His daughter didn't marry until she was forty.
他女兒直到四十歲才結婚。

marvelous
[ˋmɑrvələs]
形 了不起的

The Beatles is the most marvelous band of all time.
披頭四是有史以來最了不起的樂團。

mask
[mæsk]
名 面具

補充 performer 表演者 / stage 舞臺
All the performers on the stage wore masks.
舞臺上的所有表演者都戴著面具。

mass
[mæs]
名 大量;團;塊

補充 approve 同意、批准
The mass of the program was approved by the committee.
委員會核准了計畫中大部分的內容。

master
[ˋmæstɚ]
名 大師;主人 動 精通

He is a master of film making.
他是製作影片的大師。

mat
[mæt]
名 墊子;蓆子

補充 wipe 擦、擦淨
Please wipe your shoes on the mat before coming in.
進來前請在墊子上清清鞋子。

match
[mætʃ]
動 相配 名 比賽

The pearl necklace matches your dress perfectly.
珍珠項鍊和你的洋裝十分相襯。

math
[mæθ]
名 數學

補充 為 mathematics 的口語用法
Dad stared at me because I only got sixty points on the math test.
爸爸瞪著我,因為我數學只考了六十分。

mathematics
[ˏmæθəˋmætɪks]
名 數學

We have a mathematics exam tomorrow afternoon.
我們明天下午有數學測驗。

matter
[`mætɚ]
動 要緊 名 事情

補充 hairstyle 髮型
It doesn't matter whether you like my hairstyle or not.
你喜不喜歡我的髮型並不重要。

maximum
[`mæksəməm]
形 最大的 名 最大量

補充 exceed 超過、勝過
Drivers must not exceed a maximum of 100 kms an hour.
駕駛不得超過一百公里的最高時速。

May
[me]
名 五月

People around the world celebrate Mother's Day in May.
世界各地的人都在五月慶祝母親節。

maybe
[`mebɪ]
副 可能；也許

補充 think sth. over 認真考慮
Maybe you are right, but I still need some time to think it over.
你或許是對的，但我還是需要時間考慮一下。

meal
[mil]
名 一餐

Linda usually has an evening meal with her family on Sundays.
琳達星期天通常會和家人一起吃晚餐。

mean
[min]
動 意指 形 刻薄的

My family and friends mean everything to me.
家人與朋友是我的一切。

measure
[`mɛʒɚ]
動 測量 名 度量單位

The ruler is used to measure the length of boxes.
這把尺是用來測量盒子長度的。

meat
[mit]
名 肉類

My mother prefers vegetables to meat.
我母親喜歡吃蔬菜，勝過吃肉。

mechanic
[mə`kænɪk]
名 技工

補充 scooter 小型機車
The **mechanic** fixed my scooter.
技工修理了我的機車。

medicine
[`mɛdəsn̩]
名 藥

補充 drowsy 昏昏欲睡的 / side effect 副作用
Feeling drowsy is the side effect of the medicine.
感覺昏昏欲睡是這種藥的副作用。

medium
[`midɪəm]
形 中間的；中等的

補充 blond 金黃色的、皮膚白皙的
Josh is of medium height with blond hair.
喬許身高中等，留著一頭金髮。

meet
[mit]
動 遇見

補充 happen to 碰巧 / cinema 電影院
I happened to meet an old friend at the cinema.
我碰巧在電影院遇到一位老朋友。

member
[`mɛmbə]
名 會員

補充 lifelong 終身的 / organization 機構
Ruby is a lifelong member of this organization.
露比是這個機構的終身會員。

memory
[`mɛmərɪ]
名 記憶；記憶力

補充 remind sb. of sth. 提醒某人某事
The coffee shop reminds him of the happy memory.
這家咖啡廳讓他回想起過去的美好回憶。

men's room
片 男廁

He did not see the warning sign on the men's room.
他沒有看到男廁門口掛的警告標誌。

menu
[`mɛnju]
名 菜單

The cafeteria changes its menu every month.
這家自助餐館每個月會更新菜單。

message
[`mɛsɪdʒ]
名 訊息；消息

Someone left a message for you this afternoon.
今天下午有人留言給你。

metal
[`mɛtl]
名 金屬 形 金屬的

The metal mini car is little Ben's favorite toy.
那台金屬迷你車是小班最喜歡的玩具。

meter
[`mitɚ]
名 公尺；計量器

This balcony is 10 meters long.
這個陽臺有十公尺長。

method
[`mɛθəd]
名 方法

The student used a new method to solve the problem.
那名學生使用新的方法來解題。

metro
[`mɛtro]
名 地鐵；大都市

We looked at the map and decided to go by metro.
我們看了地圖，決定搭地鐵前往。

microwave
[`maɪkro͵wev]
名 微波爐

I think we need a new microwave to heat the food.
我認為我們需要一個新的微波爐來加熱食物。

middle
[`mɪdl]
形 中間的 名 中央

Parker is the middle child of his family.
派克在家中的排行在中間。

midnight
[`mɪd͵naɪt]
名 午夜

My father always works until midnight.
我父親總是工作到半夜。

mile
[maɪl]
名 英里

Mr. Wang used to walk two miles to school every day.
王先生以前每天走兩英里的路上學。

---

milk
[mɪlk]
名 牛奶

Danny drinks a bottle of milk every morning.
丹尼每天早上會喝一瓶牛奶。

---

million
[`mɪljən]
名 百萬

補充 fetch 去拿來、售得
The painting is expected to fetch over one million dollars.
這幅畫預計將賣出超過一百萬美元的價格。

---

mind
[maɪnd]
名 心智 動 介意

補充 brilliant 優秀的、出色的
He is a clever person with a brilliant mind.
他很聰明，有著超群的智力。

---

minor
[`maɪnɚ]
形 次要的；較少的
名 未成年者；副修科目

補充 undergo 經歷、接受（治療等）
Peter underwent a minor surgery and recovered in a few days.
彼得進行了一個小手術，在幾天內就康復了。

---

minus
[`maɪnəs]
介 減去 名 減號；負號

Seventy minus two is sixty-eight.
七十減二等於六十八。

---

minute
[`mɪnɪt]
名 分鐘

The cake will then take about 30 minutes to bake.
蛋糕接下來大概需要烤三十分鐘左右。

---

mirror
[`mɪrɚ]
名 鏡子

She stood before the mirror and could not decide which skirt is better.
她站在鏡子前，不知道哪件裙子比較好。

miss
[mɪs]
動 想念 **名** 小姐

Sandy missed her life in the countryside very much.
珊蒂很懷念她在鄉村的生活。

mistake
[mɪˋstek]
名 錯誤

He made a terrible mistake in his research paper.
他在研究報告中犯了一個嚴重的錯誤。

mix
[mɪks]
動 混合

補充 remaining 剩下的 / ingredient 原料
The chef mixed the remaining ingredients in a bowl.
主廚在碗裡混合剩餘的材料。

model
[ˋmɑdḷ]
名 模特兒；模型

Julie made her living as a model after graduation.
茱莉畢業之後以當模特兒維生。

modern
[ˋmɑdən]
形 現代的

補充 globe 球、球狀物
The modern sofa is made as a globe.
這個時髦的沙發製作成像是球體。

moment
[ˋmomənt]
名 片刻

Joe paused for a few moments before he answered the question.
在回答問題之前，喬停頓了片刻。

Monday
[ˋmʌnde]
名 星期一

Amanda got home from her trip last Monday.
亞曼達上星期一結束旅行回家。

money
[ˋmʌnɪ]
名 錢

補充 repay 償還 / interest 利息
Based on the contract, you have to repay the money with interest.
根據合約，你還錢時必須連同利息一起還。

monkey
[`mʌŋkɪ]
名 猴子

There are different kinds of monkeys by the waterfall.
瀑布旁邊有不同種類的猴子。

monster
[`mɑnstɚ]
名 怪物

補充 rumor has it that 謠傳（後接子句）
Rumor has it that there is a big monster hidden in this forest.
傳說這座森林裡藏著一個巨大的怪物。

month
[mʌnθ]
名 月份

補充 proper 適合的、恰當的
He has been trying to find a proper job for months.
他這幾個月都在試著找一份像樣的工作。

moon
[mun]
名 月亮

It was a night without moon and any star.
那是個既無月亮，也沒有星星的夜晚。

mop
[mɑp]
動 擦洗 名 拖把

補充 mop the floor 拖地
We need to mop the floor before Mom comes back.
媽媽回來之前，我們必須把地拖好。

more
[mor]
形 更多的 副 更多地
代 更多的數量

You need more practice before attending the competition.
去參加比賽之前，你需要更多的練習。

morning
[`mɔrnɪŋ]
名 早晨

補充 此處 express（名詞）指特快車
I'm taking the express at 8:30 tomorrow morning.
我會搭乘明天早上八點三十分的特快車。

mosquito
[mə`skito]
名 蚊子

We were badly bitten by mosquitoes in the forest.
我們在森林裡被蚊子叮得很厲害。

most
[most]
形 最多的　代 大部分

補充 staff 職員 / shift 輪班工作時間
Most staff in our company work shifts.
我們公司的職員大多採輪班制。

mother
[`mʌðɚ]
名 母親

補充 in an instant 立刻、馬上
The mother left her bag here and said she'll be back in an instant.
那名母親把袋子留在這裡，說她會馬上回來。

motion
[`moʃən]
名 移動

補充 work on 從事 / research 學術研究
Larry is working on a research on the motion of the planets.
賴瑞正在做行星運行的研究報告。

motorcycle
[`motɚˌsaɪkḷ]
名 機車

He traveled by motorcycle from San Francisco to San Jose.
他從舊金山騎摩托車旅行到聖荷西。

mountain
[`maʊntṇ]
名 山

We'd like to have a quiet room with a mountain view.
我們想要一間既安靜、又看得到山景的房間。

mouse
[maʊs]
名 老鼠；滑鼠

Mickey Mouse is one of the most famous cartoon characters.
米老鼠是最出名的卡通人物之一。

mouth
[maʊθ]
名 嘴巴

The boy's mouth was full of peanuts when I saw him.
我看見那個男孩時，他滿嘴都是花生。

move
[muv]
動 移動

補充 once 一旦（此處為連接詞用法）
Once the wheel is turned, you can move it easily.
只要輪子一轉，要移動它就很容易了。

movement
[`muvmənt]
名 動作；活動

補充 somehow 不知怎麼的 / clumsy 笨拙的
The little boy's movements were somehow clumsy.
不知為何，那名小男孩的動作滿笨拙的。

movie
[`muvɪ]
名 電影

補充 go to the movies 看電影
Charlie asked Amy to go to the movies with him.
查理邀請艾咪和他一起去看電影。

Mr.
[`mɪstɚ]
名 先生

補充 本單字為 mister 的縮寫
Mr. Wang has been a fan of science fiction since he was a teenager.
王先生從青少年時期開始，就是個科幻小說迷。

Mrs.
[`mɪsɪz]
名 夫人；太太

補充 對已婚女士的稱呼
Mrs. Walter arrived in the afternoon with her gifts for the children.
華特夫人下午帶著給孩子的禮物來了。

MRT
縮 大眾捷運系統

補充 完整寫法為 mass rapid transit
We went to the night market by MRT last night.
我們昨晚搭捷運去夜市。

Ms.
[mɪz]
名 女士；小姐

補充 Ms. 為不顯示女子婚姻狀況的用法
Ms. Kimberly received an honorary degree from University of Oxford.
金柏莉小姐獲頒牛津大學的榮譽學位。

much
[mʌtʃ]
形 大量的 副 非常 名 許多

According to the report, drinking too much coffee is bad for your health.
根據這份報導，喝太多咖啡對健康有害。

mud
[mʌd]
名 泥巴；爛泥

補充 crumple 弄皺 / splash 濺、潑
Kate's new skirt was crumpled and splashed with mud.
凱特的新裙子起皺，還濺到了泥巴。

museum
[`mjuˋzɪəm]
名 博物館

Every summer, the Louvre Museum would be crowded with hundreds of visitors.
每年夏天，羅浮宮都會擠滿數百名遊客。

music
[`mjuzɪk]
名 音樂

補充 fade away 漸弱、消退
The music fades away at the end of the movie.
隨著電影結束，音樂也慢慢消失。

musician
[mjuˋzɪʃən]
名 音樂家

補充 sibling 兄弟姊妹 / accomplished 有造詣的
All my siblings are accomplished musicians.
我的兄弟姊妹都是有造詣的音樂家。

must
[mʌst]
助 必須

The project must be done by next Monday.
這項計畫必須在下週一之前完成。

myself
[maɪˋsɛlf]
代 我自己（反身代名詞）

補充 stretch 伸直、舒展身體
I really need to stretch myself after sitting for a long time.
坐了這麼久，我需要伸伸懶腰。

Unit 14　Nn 字頭單字

MP3 14

nail
[nel]
名 釘子；指甲

Watch out! There is a two-inch nail on the ground.
小心！地上有根兩吋長的釘子。

name
[nem]
名 名字 動 給…命名

He keeps a puppy whose name is Lucky.
他養了一隻名叫幸運的小狗。

napkin
[`næpkɪn]
名 餐巾

Lisa went to the kitchen to get some spoons and napkins.
為了拿湯匙和餐巾，麗莎走去廚房。

narrow
[`næro]
形 窄的

You have to walk through a narrow lane to reach the park.
你必須走過一個狹窄的巷子，才會抵達公園。

nation
[`neʃən]
名 國家

補充 policy 政策、方針
The President announced a new policy to the nation.
總統向全國國民宣布一項新政策。

national
[`næʃənḷ]
形 國家的

Many people consider baseball to be a national sport in Taiwan.
很多人視棒球為臺灣的國民運動。

natural
[`nætʃərəl]
形 天然的；自然的

補充 product 產品
All the ingredients we use for our products are natural.
所有我們用於產品的原料都是天然的。

nature
[`netʃɚ]
名 自然

補充 wildlife 野生動植物
Chris shows great interest in nature and wildlife.
克里斯對自然與野外生活展現出莫大的興趣。

naughty
[`nɔtɪ]
形 頑皮的

補充 be strict with 對…嚴厲
Tom is such a naughty boy. You should be strict with him.
湯姆是個頑皮的孩子，你應該對他嚴格一點。

near
[nɪr]
介 在…附近
形 近的　副 幾乎

補充 counter 櫃檯
The counter is near the entrance, next to the elevator.
櫃檯位於入口附近，在電梯旁邊。

necessary
[`nɛsə͵sɛrɪ]
形 需要的；必要的

It's necessary for kids to learn another language.
對小孩來說，學習另外一種語言是必要的。

neck
[nɛk]
名 脖子

Last night, Fiona wore her new necklace around her neck.
昨晚，費歐娜戴上了她的新項鍊。

necklace
[`nɛklɪs]
名 項鍊

We returned the diamond necklace to the lady.
我們把鑽石項鍊歸還給那位小姐。

need
[nid]
動 名 需要

The cake is too sweet, so I need a cup of tea to go with it.
蛋糕太甜了，我需要一杯茶配著吃。

needle
[`nidl̩]
名 針

補充 thread a needle 穿針
Can you thread this needle for me?
你能幫我把線穿過這根針嗎？

negative
[`nɛgətɪv]
形 否定的；負面的

To my surprise, her answer was negative.
讓我驚訝的是，她給了否定的答案。

neighbor
[`nebɚ]
名 鄰居

Our neighbor gave us a ride home from the supermarket.
鄰居開車把我們從超市載回家。

neither
[ˋniðɚ]
連 也不 副 也不
形 兩者都不

Neither Tom nor I was interested in this musical.
我跟湯姆對這齣音樂劇都不感興趣。

nephew
[ˋnɛfju]
名 侄子；外甥

My nephew likes cartoons and comics very much.
我姪子很喜歡卡通和漫畫。

nervous
[ˋnɝvəs]
形 緊張的

補充 give sb. a shot 幫某人打針
The boy looked nervous when the nurse gave him a shot.
當護士打針時，男孩看起來很緊張。

nest
[nɛst]
名 鳥巢

We saw an eagle's nest on the rocks.
我們在岩石上看到一個老鷹的鳥巢。

net
[nɛt]
名 網子

補充 stick, stuck, stuck 被困住
There is a tennis ball stuck in the net.
有一顆網球卡在網子裡。

never
[ˋnɛvɚ]
副 永不；從來沒有

The price of the product has never changed before.
這個商品的價格以前從未變過。

new
[nju]
形 新的

We are going to move into a new house next week.
我們下星期要搬去新房屋。

news
[njuz]
名 新聞

The latest sports news will be at nine on ESPN Sports Channel.
最新的體育新聞九點會在 ESPN 體育台播出。

newspaper
[`njuz͵pepɚ]
名 報紙

The newspaper has sales of 1.3 million.
這份報紙有一百三十萬份的銷售量。

next
[nɛkst]
形 下一個的；其次的

My science teacher would give us a test next Wednesday.
我的自然老師下星期三要給我們小考。

nice
[naɪs]
形 好的；善良的

The nice girl helped the dog get out of the hole.
那個善良的女孩幫助小狗從坑洞裡爬出來。

nice-looking
[͵naɪs`lukɪŋ]
形 好看的

Did you see her boyfriend? What a nice-looking guy.
你有看到她男友嗎？長得真帥氣。

niece
[nis]
名 侄女；外甥女

補充 adopt 收養、採納
She adopted her ten-year-old niece after her brother's death.
在哥哥過世後，她收養了十歲的姪女。

night
[naɪt]
名 夜晚

補充 comedian 喜劇演員
The comedian made the audience laugh a lot last night.
昨晚，那名喜劇演員讓觀眾笑得很開心。

nine
[naɪn]
形 九的 名 九

補充 hometown 故鄉、家鄉
Johnny hasn't gone back to his hometown for nine years.
強尼已經九年沒回家鄉了。

nineteen
[`naɪn`tin]
形 十九的 名 十九

補充 bargain 特價商品
This dress is quite a bargain; it only costs nineteen US dollars.
這件洋裝很划算，只賣十九美元。

ninety
[`naɪntɪ]
形 九十的 名 九十

補充 pamphlet 小冊子
The pamphlet she gave me has ninety pages in total.
她給我的這本冊子總共有九十頁。

no
[no]
形 沒有；不 副 一點也不

補充 candidate 候選人、應試者
The first candidate is a graduate with no experience at all.
第一位應試者是個毫無經驗的畢業生。

nobody
[`no͵bɑdɪ]
代 沒有人 名 無名小卒

I'm afraid that nobody would believe me.
我害怕沒有人會相信我。

nod
[nɑd]
動 名 點頭

The teacher nodded and then left the classroom.
老師點點頭，離開了教室。

noise
[nɔɪz]
名 噪音

補充 concentrate on 專注於…
There was so much noise that I couldn't concentrate on my reading.
噪音實在太吵，導致我無法專心閱讀。

noisy
[`nɔɪzɪ]
形 喧鬧的

Mr. and Mrs. Thomas' son was very noisy in the mornings.
湯瑪斯夫婦的兒子早上會非常吵鬧。

none
[nʌn]
代 無一（人或物）；毫無

補充 approve of 贊成
None of her family members approved of their marriage.
她的家人當中，沒有人贊成他們的婚事。

noodle
[`nudl̩]
名 麵；麵條

Jennifer wants rice for lunch rather than noodles.
珍妮佛午餐想吃飯而不是麵。

noon
[nun]
名 中午

Sarah and I will meet at noon for lunch.
莎拉和我中午會碰面，一起吃午餐。

nor
[nɔr]
連 也不

補充 neither A nor B 兩者皆不⋯
Neither Lisa nor Frank can solve this math problem.
不只麗莎，連法蘭克也無法解出這道數學問題。

north
[nɔrθ]
副 向北方
形 北方的 名 北方

補充 for a while 一會兒
Keep driving north for a while, and turn right after the mall.
往北再開一會兒，看到購物中心後右轉。

nose
[noz]
名 鼻子

補充 have a runny nose 流鼻水
Cindy got a runny nose because she caught a cold.
辛蒂因為感冒而流鼻涕。

not
[nɑt]
副 不

補充 protection 保護、防護
It concerns me that those children do not get proper protection.
我擔心那些孩子們沒有受到適當的保護。

note
[not]
名 筆記 動 注意

補充 in case 後面直接加子句
He prepared a note to read in case he is too nervous.
他準備了一張小抄，萬一太緊張可以照著念。

notebook
[`not, buk]
名 筆記本；筆記型電腦

補充 exquisite 精美的
Tiffany's birthday gift is an exquisite notebook.
蒂芬妮的生日禮物是一本精美的筆記本。

nothing
[`nʌθɪŋ]
代 無事；無物

There was nothing in the cupboard except a bowl.
櫥櫃裡什麼都沒有，只有一個碗。

notice
[`notɪs]
名 布告；通知 動 注意到

They posted up a notice this morning.
他們今天早上張貼了一則布告。

novel
[`nɑvḷ]
名 小說

補充 in one's spare time 某人的空閒時間
Jenny likes to write novels during her spare time.
珍妮空閒時喜歡寫小說。

November
[no`vɛmbɚ]
名 十一月

The musical is going to play from October 1 to November 2.
這齣音樂劇的上演日是從十月一日到十一月二日。

now
[naʊ]
副 現在

Doris is busy now, so it's better not to bother her.
朵莉絲現在正在忙，所以最好不要打擾她。

number
[`nʌmbɚ]
名 號碼；數字

He took a number and found a seat, waiting to be called.
他拿了號碼牌，接著便找座位等候叫號。

nurse
[nɜs]
名 護士

補充 inject sth. into 將藥液注射進…
The nurse injected the drug into the girl's arm.
護士把藥注射進女孩的手臂。

nut
[nʌt]
名 堅果

補充 a handful of 一把
It is good for your health to eat a handful of nuts every day.
每天吃一把堅果有益健康。

Unit 15 Oo 字頭單字

MP3 15

obey
[ə`be]
動 遵守；服從

補充 military 軍隊 / regulation 規章
In the military, you have to obey the regulations and orders.
在軍隊中，你必須遵守規定與命令。

object
[`abdʒɪkt]
名 物品 動 反對

補充 當動詞時的音標為 [əb`dʒɛkt]
There are too many objects in the room.
房間裡有太多物品了。

ocean
[`oʃən]
名 海洋

There are all kinds of animals in the ocean.
海洋中有各式各樣的動物。

o'clock
[ə`klak]
名 …點鐘

The train should arrive at 12 o'clock on platform 2.
火車會在十二點鐘抵達二號月臺。

October
[ak`tobɚ]
名 十月

補充 parade 遊行
They decorated the streets for the parade in October.
他們為十月份的遊行布置街道。

of
[əv]
介 …的；屬於

補充 memorize 背熟
He memorized the words of Abraham Lincoln's famous speech.
他背下林肯著名演說的內容。

off
[ɔf]
副 離開 形 離開的
介 離開；去掉

補充 force 強迫 / lay off 解僱
The company has been forced to lay off fifty employees.
那間公司被迫解僱了五十名員工。

offer
[`ɔfɚ]
動 提供

補充 take one's temperature 量某人體溫
She took the boy's temperature and offered him some water.
她為男孩量體溫，並給他喝些水。

office
[`ɔfɪs]
名 辦公室

Ms. Hill will arrive at the office at ten in the morning.
希爾小姐早上十點會到辦公室。

officer
[`ɔfɪsɚ]
名 軍官；官員

補充 in vain 徒勞的 / contact 聯絡
We tried in vain to get into contact with that officer.
我們試圖聯絡那位官員，但沒有成功。

often
[`ɔfən]
副 常常

It often rains in the afternoon during summer in Taiwan.
臺灣的夏日午後經常下雨。

oil
[ɔɪl]
名 油

補充 disaster 災難 / creature 生物
The oil spill was a disaster which caused a lot of creatures' death.
那次漏油是一場災難，造成大量生物死亡。

OK/O.K/okay
[o`ke]
名 好；沒問題 形 好的

補充 explanation 解釋
Her explanation was OK for the teacher.
老師覺得她的解釋還可以接受。

old
[old]
形 年老的

補充 incredibly 難以置信地、極為
Those 10-year-old children are incredibly energetic.
那群十歲的孩童精力非常旺盛。

omit
[o`mɪt]
動 忽略不做；省略

She omitted reading the less important chapter in the book.
她跳過書中較不重要的一章沒有閱讀。

on
[ɑn]
介 在…上面

補充 wallpaper 壁紙
Tina likes the pattern on that wallpaper.
蒂娜喜歡那款壁紙上的花色。

once
[wʌns]
副 一次;曾經

I don't know him. I only met him once before.
我不認識他,我之前只見過他一次。

one
[wʌn]
形 一個的
名 一個(人、事、物)

They have been living together for more than one year.
他們已經住在一起超過一年了。

oneself
[wʌn`sɛlf]
代 自己(反身代名詞)

One should learn to control oneself.
人必須學會控制自己。

onion
[`ʌnjən]
名 洋蔥

They ordered fried chicken and onion rings to go.
他們點了炸雞和洋蔥圈外帶。

only
[`onlɪ]
副 只;僅僅 連 可是;若非

補充 relative 親戚(名)、相對的(形)
She only invited close friends and relatives to her wedding.
她僅邀請親近的朋友和親戚參加婚禮。

open
[`opən]
動 打開

Nancy opened the door, and greeted her boyfriend with a smile.
南西去開門,以微笑迎接她的男友。

operation
[ˌɑpə`reʃən]
名 操作;手術

補充 manual 手冊、簡介
I read the manual to know the operation of the copy machine.
我閱讀說明書,以了解影印機的操作方法。

opinion
[əˋpɪnjən]
名 意見；主張

補充 humble 謙遜的、謙恭的
This is just my humble opinion.
這只是我的淺見。

or
[ɔr]
連 或者；否則

Do you like beef or pork?
你喜歡牛肉還是豬肉？

orange
[ˋɔrɪndʒ]
名 柳橙 形 橘色的

補充 jug 指餐廳常見的那種水罐容器
Is there any orange juice in the jug?
罐子裡還有柳橙汁嗎？

order
[ˋɔrdɚ]
名 訂單 動 點菜；訂購

補充 take (one's) order 替某人點餐
The waiter came to take our order.
服務生走過來替我們點餐。

ordinary
[ˋɔrdn͵ɛrɪ]
形 平常的；普通的

He's just an ordinary man. Don't
expect too much from him.
他只是普通人，不要對他期望太高。

other
[ˋʌðɚ]
形 其他的 代 其他人或物

There is no sense in fighting with
each other now.
現在互相爭吵一點好處也沒有。

our
[aur]
限 我們的（所有格）

補充 ours 我們的（東西）
Our interests and hobbies are
exactly the same.
我們的興趣和嗜好一模一樣。

out
[aut]
副 向外 形 在外的
介 通過…而去

I am not going out tonight because
I feel very tired.
我今天晚上不想出門，因為我非常累。

outside
[`aʊt`saɪd]
介 在…外面　副 在外面

補充 vending machine 自動販賣機
There is a vending machine outside **the classroom.**
在教室外面有個自動販賣機。

oven
[`ʌvən]
名 烤箱

補充 preheat 預先加熱
Before you put your food in the oven, make sure you preheat it.
將食物放進去烤之前，記得先預熱烤箱。

over
[`ovɚ]
副 超過　形 結束的
介 在…上方

補充 the Pacific Ocean 太平洋
The treasure was sunk in the Atlantic for over **300 years.**
那寶藏沉在大西洋中有三百多年的時間了。

overpass
[`ovɚ͵pæs]
名 天橋

They walked across the road through an overpass.
他們走天橋穿越道路。

overseas
[͵ovɚ`siz]
副 在海外　形 國外的

He has been traveling overseas **to serve the needy.**
他一直在海外為貧困人士服務。

overweight
[`ovɚ͵wet]
形 超重的；過重的

Being overweight **would increase your risk of getting heart disease.**
體重過重，得心臟病的可能性就變高。

own
[on]
形 自己的　動 擁有

補充 ignore 忽視 / on one's own 獨自
She ignored others' advice and ran into the forest on her own.
她不顧其他人的忠告，獨自跑進森林裡。

owner
[`onɚ]
名 持有者；擁有者

Jeff is the owner **of this grocery store.**
傑夫是這家雜貨店的老闆。

ox
[ɑks]
名 公牛

An ox can be both gentle and dangerous.
公牛可以很溫馴，也可以很危險。

Pp 字頭單字

MP3 16

P.M./p.m.
副 下午

The regular opening hours of library are 9 a.m. to 8 p.m.
圖書館平日開放時間為早上九點至晚上八點。

pack
[pæk]
動 打包 名 一包

補充 eliminate 淘汰 / belongings 財產
The girl who was eliminated is packing her belongings.
被淘汰的女孩正在收拾行李。

package
[`pækɪdʒ]
名 包裹

補充 on the way home 在回家的路上
We bought a package of doughnuts on the way home.
回家路上，我們買了一盒甜甜圈。

page
[pedʒ]
名 書頁

How many birds are there in the big tree on this page?
這一頁的大樹上畫有幾隻鳥呢？

pain
[pen]
名 疼痛；痛苦

My grandfather's back gives him a lot of pain.
我爺爺背痛得厲害。

painful
[`penfəl]
形 疼痛的；痛苦的

補充 scandal 醜聞、醜事
It must be painful for the victim to talk about the scandal.
對受害者而言，談論這樁醜聞想必很痛苦。

paint
[pent]
動 畫圖；油漆

補充 relieve 緩和、減輕
To me, painting is a good way to relieve stress.
對我來說，繪畫是抒發壓力的好方式。

painter
[`pentɚ]
名 畫家

The painter likes to use light colors.
這名畫家喜歡使用明亮的顏色。

pair
[pɛr]
名 一對；一副 動 配成對

Sunny bought a pair of shoes for her mother.
桑妮買了一雙鞋子給她母親。

pajamas
[pə`dʒɑməz]
名 睡衣

The girl walked downstairs and was still in pajamas.
女孩走下樓來，還穿著睡衣。

pale
[pel]
形 蒼白的；黯淡的

The nurse looked pale and tired after the night shift.
這名護士值完夜班後，看起來蒼白又疲倦。

pan
[pæn]
名 平底鍋

補充 garlic 大蒜
Heat the garlic and oil in a large pan.
在一個大平底鍋裡加熱大蒜和油。

panda
[`pændə]
名 貓熊

補充 biologist 生物學家
The biologist observed the panda to see how it would react to the test.
生物學家觀察貓熊對測驗的反應。

pants
[pænts]
名 褲子

Julia bought a new pair of pants for her son.
茱莉亞買了一條新褲子給她兒子。

papaya
[pə`paɪə]
名 木瓜

Papayas can be made into juice, and they are also often used in cooking.
木瓜可以打成果汁，也經常用於烹飪。

paper
[`pepɚ]
名 紙張

補充 director 導演
The director wrote something on the blank paper.
導演在空白紙上寫了一些東西。

pardon
[`pɑrdn̩]
動 寬恕；原諒

補充 catch up with sth./sb. 趕上…
Pardon me. I was in a hurry to catch up with the bus.
請原諒我，我那時正趕著去搭車。

parent
[`pɛrənt]
名 雙親；家長

補充 association 協會、聯盟
William goes to the single-parent association every Friday.
威廉每週五都去單親協會。

park
[pɑrk]
名 公園 動 停車

The weather was so good that many people came to the park to picnic.
天氣超好，許多人都來公園野餐。

parking lot
片 停車場

補充 as long as 只要…就…（條件句）
You may use our parking lot as long as you have a pass.
只要有通行證，你就能使用我們的停車場。

parrot
[`pærət]
名 鸚鵡

補充 flight（飛鳥的）群
A flight of parrots just flew out from the forest.
一群鸚鵡剛從森林裡飛出來。

part
[part]
名 部分

The major part of the customers in our restaurant prefers the new menu.
我們餐廳大部分的顧客偏好新菜單。

partner
[`partnɚ]
名 夥伴

My partner for the math competition is Terry.
我在數學競賽上的搭檔是泰瑞。

party
[`partɪ]
名 派對

Pink is never the pick for her party dress.
她從不穿粉紅色服裝去參加派對。

pass
[pæs]
動 經過；傳遞

補充 pass away 過世（委婉語）
I have a feeling that I can pass the exam.
我感覺自己會通過這場考試。

passenger
[`pæsṇdʒɚ]
名 乘客

We have to check every passenger's temperature before boarding.
所有乘客在登機前都必須量體溫。

past
[pæst]
形 過去的
名 過去 介 經過

For the past five years, he stayed in southern Taiwan.
過去五年，他都待在南臺灣。

paste
[pest]
動 貼上 名 漿糊

補充 left-hand 左側的、左邊的
The "paste" icon is on the top left-hand corner of the window.
「貼上」圖示在視窗的左上角。

path
[pæθ]
名 小徑；路徑

補充 tornado 龍捲風 / predict 預料
The path of the tornado is hard to predict.
龍捲風的路線難以預測。

patient
[`peʃənt]
名 病人 形 有耐心的

補充 helplessly 無力地、無助地
The patient looked at the doctor helplessly.
病人無助地看著醫生。

pattern
[`pætən]
名 圖案;模式

補充 jasmine 茉莉花
My sister wore a dress with a pattern of jasmines on it.
我姐姐穿著有茉莉花圖案的洋裝。

pause
[pɔz]
動 名 暫停;中斷

The musician missed a pause here.
那位音樂家遺漏了這裡的一個延長記號。

pay
[pe]
動 付錢 名 工資

補充 front desk 櫃檯、服務檯
Mr. Watson went to the front desk and paid the bill.
華森先生走去櫃檯付帳。

peace
[pis]
名 和平

補充 meditation 冥想
Meditation brings us inner peace and happiness.
冥想帶給我內心的平靜與快樂。

peaceful
[`pisfəl]
形 和平的;安寧的

補充 neighborhood 近鄰、街坊
It is very peaceful in this neighborhood.
這附近相當寧靜。

peach
[pitʃ]
名 桃子

補充 plum 李子
My mother prefers peaches to plums.
比起李子,我媽媽比較喜歡桃子。

pear
[pɛr]
名 梨子

補充 in season 當令的、當季的
We bought pears because they are now in season.
我們買了梨子,因為是當季水果。

pen
[pɛn]
名 原子筆

May I borrow your pen?
我可以借用你的原子筆嗎？

---

pencil
[`pɛnsḷ]
名 鉛筆

補充 landscape 景色 / sketch 素描
She had drawn a landscape sketch in pencil.
她已經用鉛筆畫了一張風景草圖。

---

people
[`pipḷ]
名 人們

補充 considerate 體貼的、考慮周到的
He is considerate, so many people like him.
他很體貼，所以很多人喜歡他。

---

pepper
[`pɛpɚ]
名 胡椒；辣椒

補充 cook 廚師 / cooker 廚具
Jennifer passed the cook the pepper.
珍妮佛把胡椒遞給廚師。

---

perfect
[`pɝfɪkt]
形 完美的

補充 decline 減少
The house price is declining, so it is the perfect time to buy a house.
房價正在下跌，所以現在是買房的最佳時機。

---

perhaps
[pɚ`hæps]
副 或許；可能

補充 be meant to be together 天生一對
Perhaps you are meant to be together.
或許你們是天生一對吧！

---

period
[`pɪrɪəd]
名 期間；週期

補充 hold one's breath 憋氣、屏住呼吸
Brittney can hold her breath for a long period of time.
布蘭妮可以憋氣很長一段時間。

---

person
[`pɝsṇ]
名 人

補充 複數形為 people
I am not sure that he is the kind of person to steal.
我不覺得他是會偷竊的那種人。

personal
[`pɜsənḷ]
形 個人的

She does an excellent job as Steve's personal assistant.
她擔任史蒂夫的私人助理，做得非常稱職。

---

pet
[pɛt]
名 寵物

Victor's daughter keeps a cat as her pet.
維克多的女兒養了一隻貓當寵物。

---

phone
[fon]
名 電話

補充 make a phone call 打電話
Please write your phone number here.
請把你的電話號碼寫在這裡。

---

photo
[`foto]
名 相片

This photo shows four of the eight planets in the solar system.
這張照片顯示太陽系八大行星中的四顆。

---

physics
[`fɪzɪks]
名 物理學

At that time, only a small group of people studied physics.
當時，只有少數人攻讀物理學。

---

piano
[pɪ`æno]
名 鋼琴

There were about 100 people seeing him playing the piano.
大約有一百人看他彈奏鋼琴。

---

pick
[pɪk]
動 挑選；採收；撿起

補充 pick sb. up 接某人
The ladies hold the right to pick their dancing partners.
女士享有選擇舞伴的權利。

---

picnic
[`pɪknɪk]
名 野餐

補充 go on a picnic 去野餐
In summer, we like to go on a picnic in the park.
我們喜歡在夏天的時候去公園野餐。

171

picture
[`pɪktʃɚ]
名 圖畫;照片

補充 still 靜止的、不動的
If you kept still, I can draw a picture of you more quickly.
如果你不動的話,我就能更快畫好你的畫像。

pie
[paɪ]
名 派(食品)

補充 homemade 自製的
Adam loves his mother's homemade strawberry pie.
亞當非常喜歡他媽媽親手做的草莓派。

piece
[pis]
名 一件;一片

補充 be made of 由…做的(看得出原料)
This fine piece of furniture is made of solid wood.
這件精緻的傢俱是用實木製成的。

pig
[pɪg]
名 豬

Those pigs are covered in mud.
那些豬全身都是泥巴。

pigeon
[`pɪdʒɪn]
名 鴿子

補充 coo(鴿子等)咕咕地叫
Three pigeons were cooing up on the lawn.
三隻鴿子在草地上咕咕叫。

pile
[paɪl]
名 一堆 動 堆積

He has a pile of clothes to wash today.
他今天有一堆衣服要洗。

pillow
[`pɪlo]
名 枕頭

This pillow is too soft. I need a harder one.
這個枕頭太軟了。我需要一個硬一點的。

pin
[pɪn]
名 大頭針;胸針

補充 fund-raising 募款的
In the fund-raising party, every guest wore a red ribbon pin.
募款會上的每位賓客都別上了紅絲帶的別針。

pineapple
[`paɪnˌæpḷ]
名 鳳梨

Nina had some pineapple juice by the beach.
妮娜在海灘邊喝了一些鳳梨汁。

pink
[pɪŋk]
形 粉紅色的 名 粉紅色

His aunt dressed in pink even if she is over 50 years old.
即使已經年過五十，他嬸嬸仍穿粉紅色的衣服。

pipe
[paɪp]
名 煙斗；管子

補充 tamp 填塞 / wad 一團 / tobacco 菸草
Grandpa tamped a wad of tobacco into his pipe.
爺爺將一團菸草塞進他的菸斗裡。

pizza
[`pitsə]
名 披薩

Emily cut the pizza into eight equal sections.
艾蜜莉把披薩切成八等份。

place
[ples]
名 地點 動 放置

Sally knows a good place to study.
莎莉知道一個適合讀書的好地點。

plain
[plen]
形 明白的；平坦的 名 平原

It was a plain and simple step to follow.
那是一個明白簡單，又容易執行的步驟。

plan
[plæn]
動 計劃 名 計畫

補充 voucher 票券
She plans to shop for cosmetics with the consumer vouchers.
她打算用消費券購買化妝品。

plane
[plen]
名 飛機

補充 take off 起飛 / land 降落
Once all passengers are seated, the plane will take off.
一旦所有乘客坐定，飛機就起飛。

planet
[`plænɪt]
名 行星

Jupiter is the biggest planet in the solar system.
木星是太陽系裡最大的行星。

plant
[plænt]
名 植物；工廠
動 栽種；播種

Could you take care of my plants during my holidays?
你可以在我度假期間幫我照顧植物嗎？

plate
[plet]
名 盤子；碟子

She cut the tomatoes and placed them on a beautiful plate.
她切好番茄，並放在一個漂亮的盤子上。

platform
[`plæt,fɔrm]
名 月臺；平台

補充 depart 出發、離開
The train for Manchester will depart from platform five.
開往曼徹斯特的火車將從第五月臺離開。

play
[ple]
動 玩 名 遊戲；戲劇

補充 yawn 打呵欠
He keeps yawning because he played computer games all night.
由於打了整晚的電腦遊戲，他一直打呵欠。

player
[`pleə]
名 運動員；表演者

補充 claim 聲稱、主張
The players threw the caps high in the air to claim their victory.
隊員們把帽子丟向空中，迎接勝利。

playground
[`ple,graund]
名 運動場；遊樂場

My nieces ran and played in the playground all afternoon.
我的姪女們整個下午都在遊樂場奔跑玩耍。

pleasant
[`plɛznt]
形 令人愉快的；美好的

It's a pleasant weather which makes us want to go swimming.
這麼好的天氣讓我們想去游泳。

please
[pliz]
感 請 動 取悅

補充 notify sb. of sth. 通知某人某件事
Please notify the members of the news.
請通知成員們這件消息。

pleased
[plizd]
形 欣喜的

補充 be able to 能夠
We are so pleased that you are able to come to our wedding.
我們很高興你能來參加我們的婚禮。

pleasure
[`plɛʒə]
名 愉快；高興

It has been a great pleasure to work with you.
與你共事是一件愉快的事。

plus
[plʌs]
介 加上 名 正號

Eight plus seven equals fifteen.
八加七等於十五。

pocket
[`pɑkɪt]
名 口袋

The man stood there with his right hand in his pocket.
那名男士右手插著口袋，站在那裡。

poem
[`poɪm]
名 詩

補充 compose 作詩、作曲
The students were asked to compose a poem in class.
學生被要求在課堂上作一首詩。

point
[pɔɪnt]
名 要點；得分
動 指向；瞄準

補充 illustrate 說明、闡明
The following example will illustrate my point clearly.
下面的例子將能清楚地解釋我的論點。

poison
[`pɔɪzn]
動 下毒 名 毒藥

The king was poisoned by one of the princes.
國王被其中一名王子毒害。

police
[pəˋlis]
名 警察

There is a police station around the corner.
在轉角處有一間警局。

polite
[pəˋlaɪt]
形 有禮貌的

補充 chat with sb. 與某人聊天
She had a good time chatting with the polite young man.
她和那位有禮的年輕人聊得很愉快。

pollute
[pəˋlut]
動 汙染

補充 oil spill 油輪漏油
The sea was polluted by the oil spill.
海洋被漏油給汙染了。

pollution
[pəˋluʃən]
名 汙染

補充 environmental 環境的
Recycling helps control environmental pollution.
資源回收能幫助控制環境汙染的問題。

pond
[pɑnd]
名 池塘

補充 fish 釣魚 / trout 鱒魚
The man fished the pond for trout.
男子在這個池塘裡釣鱒魚。

pool
[pul]
名 水池

Jim goes to the swimming pool once a week.
吉姆每週都去一次游泳池。

poor
[pʊr]
形 貧窮的

The poor man didn't have any money.
那個貧窮的男子身無分文。

pop
[pɑp]
形 流行的；大眾的
名 流行音樂

Alice wants to be a pop singer like Lady Gaga.
艾莉絲想成為像女神卡卡一樣的流行歌手。

pop music
片 流行音樂

He will always be remembered in the world of pop music.
他在流行音樂界會永遠被記得。

popcorn
[`pɑp,kɔrn]
名 爆米花

Popcorn is a necessity to me when I see a movie.
看電影的時候，爆米花對我來說是必備的。

popular
[`pɑpjələ]
形 流行的；受歡迎的

What is the most popular activity here?
這裡最受歡迎的活動是什麼呢？

population
[,pɑpjə`leʃən]
名 人口

The population of this city is over one million.
這座城市的人口超過一百萬。

pork
[pɔrk]
名 豬肉

Which does Jenny like, pork or chicken?
珍妮喜歡哪一樣，豬肉或雞肉？

position
[pə`zɪʃən]
名 位置

He drew a line on the floor to mark the position of the sofa.
他在地板上畫了一條線，標示沙發的位置。

positive
[`pɑzətɪv]
形 正面的；積極的

補充 attitude 態度 / negative 消極的
Lisa has a positive attitude towards the new task.
麗莎對這個新任務抱持著積極的態度。

possible
[`pɑsəbḷ]
形 可能的

Is it possible to get the ticket for the concert?
有可能買到這場演唱會的票嗎？

177

post
[post]
動 貼出布告;郵寄
名 郵政;崗位

You must obey the speed limit posted on signs along the roads.
開車時必須遵守路邊標誌所公布的速限。

post office
片 郵局

補充 wrap 包、裹
He wrapped the boxes and brought them to the post office.
他包好箱子,帶去郵局。

postcard
[`post,kard]
名 明信片

My friend sent me a postcard from England three weeks ago.
三週前,我朋友從英國寄來一張明信片。

pot
[pat]
名 壺;鍋

We need to put the seed in a water pot for hours first.
我們必須先把種子泡在水罐裡好幾個小時。

potato
[pə`teto]
名 馬鈴薯

補充 steam 蒸(動詞)、蒸氣(名詞)
The cook pounded the steamed potato for dinner.
為了準備晚餐,廚師把蒸熟的馬鈴薯搗碎。

pound
[paund]
名 磅 動 重擊

He gained 10 pounds after he got married.
結婚後,他的體重增加了十磅。

powder
[`paudə]
名 粉;粉末 動 灑粉

補充 sack 粗布袋、麻袋
What is the powder in the sack?
麻袋裡裝的是什麼粉?

power
[`pauə]
名 權力;力量

He doesn't have the power to cancel our meeting.
他沒有權力取消我們的會議。

practice
[`præktɪs]
動 名 練習

The best way of learning English is to practice it every day.
學英文的最佳方式就是每天練習。

praise
[prez]
動 讚美

補充 outstanding 傑出的
The teacher praised Daniel for his outstanding performance.
老師讚美丹尼爾的傑出表現。

pray
[pre]
動 禱告

補充 safely 安全地、平安地
We prayed that he could come back safely.
我們祈禱他能平安回來。

precious
[`prɛʃəs]
形 寶貴的；珍貴的

補充 border 給…鑲邊 / jewel 寶石
The crown is bordered with precious jewels.
王冠鑲滿了貴重的珠寶。

prepare
[prɪ`pɛr]
動 準備

Don't bother Albert; he is preparing for the exam.
不要打擾亞伯特，他正在準備考試。

present
[`prɛznt]
名 禮物 動 提出

補充 當動詞時，音標為 [prɪ`zɛnt]
Ivy did not like her birthday present at all.
艾薇一點也不喜歡她的生日禮物。

president
[`prɛzədənt]
名 校長；總統

補充 document 文件
The president spent the entire morning signing the documents.
總統整個早上都在簽署文件。

pressure
[`prɛʃɚ]
名 壓力

補充 vomit 嘔吐
Stop giving me pressure. I feel like vomiting
別再給我壓力，我感覺快吐了。

pretty
[`prɪtɪ]
形 漂亮的 副 十分地；相當

Mia is a pretty and polite girl. We all like to talk to her.
米亞是一位漂亮又有禮貌的女孩，我們都很喜歡和她聊天。

price
[praɪs]
名 價格

She offered a lower price but did not interest the buyer.
她出了一個較低的價格，但並沒有引起買家的興趣。

priest
[prist]
名 牧師；神父

補充 suffer from 受苦、患病
The old priest suffered from Alzheimer in recent years.
這幾年，老神父深受失智症所苦。

primary
[`praɪˏmɛrɪ]
形 主要的；初級的

補充 mission 任務、使命
The primary mission is to build schools and provide clean water.
最重要的任務就是建校與提供乾淨的水。

prince
[prɪns]
名 王子

補充 recognize 認出、識別
The prince was surprised that nobody recognized him.
令王子訝異的是，竟沒人認出他。

princess
[`prɪnsɪs]
名 公主

Christine is playing the part of the princess in our play.
克莉斯汀在我們這齣劇中扮演公主的角色。

principal
[`prɪnsəpḷ]
名 校長；資本

Mr. Watson becomes the principal of our university.
華森先生成為我們的大學校長。

principle
[`prɪnsəpḷ]
名 原則；主義

補充 in accordance with 符合
Angela does everything in accordance with her principle.
安潔拉依照自己的原則行事。

print
[prɪnt]
動 印刷

The book is printed on environmentally-friendly paper.
這本書使用環保紙印刷。

---

printer
[`prɪntɚ]
名 印表機

補充 run out of 用完；耗盡
The laser printer in the office ran out of blue ink.
辦公室裡的雷射印表機沒有藍色墨水了。

---

private
[`praɪvɪt]
形 私密的；私人的

Mr. Anderson owns a private hospital.
安德森先生擁有一間私人醫院。

---

prize
[praɪz]
名 獎品

Rebecca won the first prize in the speech competition.
芮貝卡在演講比賽中獲得第一名。

---

problem
[`prɑbləm]
名 問題

補充 connection 連接；聯結
There seems to be a problem with our connection.
我們的網路連線似乎有問題。

---

produce
[prə`djus]
動 製造 **名** 農產品

補充 當名詞使用時，音標為 [`prɑdjus]
The waste paper and bottles can be recycled to produce again.
廢紙和瓶子能被回收，再次用於生產。

---

production
[prə`dʌkʃən]
名 製造；生產

補充 meet the demand 滿足需求
The daily production could not meet the demand in the wartime.
每日的生產量不足以應付戰時的需求。

---

professor
[prə`fɛsɚ]
名 教授

補充 go mad 發瘋、失去理智
You'd better complete your essay before the professor goes mad.
你最好趕快在教授發飆前完成你的論文。

program
[`progræm]
名 節目

補充 tribe 部落、村莊
The program visited many tribes in South America.
這個節目造訪了許多南美洲的部落。

progress
[`pragrɛs]
名 進步

補充 be in progress 進行中
The project is in progress and everything is going well so far.
這個專案已經在進行中，目前一切順利。

project
[`pradʒɛkt]
名 計畫

補充 little 不多的 / a little 稍許的
He was assigned a project of little importance.
他被分配到一個不重要的專案。

promise
[`pramɪs]
動 承諾；約定 名 諾言

補充 brief 簡略的、簡短的
Do you have a minute to talk? I promise I'll be brief.
你有時間和我談一下嗎？我保證很快就結束。

pronounce
[prə`nauns]
動 發音

Have I pronounced your name correctly?
我有念對你的名字嗎？

protect
[prə`tɛkt]
動 保護

補充 bodyguard 保鑣、護衛者
Don't worry. The bodyguard will protect you.
別擔心，保鑣會保護你。

proud
[praud]
形 驕傲的；感到光榮的

補充 be proud of 以⋯為榮
Ms. Lee is very proud of her daughter.
李小姐很以她的女兒為榮。

provide
[prə`vaɪd]
動 提供；供應

Our school provided some self-learning programs.
我們學校提供了一些自學課程。

public
[`pʌblɪk]
名 公眾 形 公開的；公立的

The auction is open to the general public.
這場拍賣會開放給一般大眾參加。

pull
[pʊl]
動 名 拉；拖

Hans pulled the chair to the fire.
漢斯將椅子拉到火堆旁。

pump
[pʌmp]
動 抽水；打氣 名 抽水機

They pumped water out of the flooded basement.
他們將水抽出遭淹沒的地下室。

pumpkin
[`pʌmpkɪn]
名 南瓜

People use pumpkins to make jack-o'-lanterns during Halloween.
萬聖節時，人們會用南瓜製成南瓜燈。

punish
[`pʌnɪʃ]
動 處罰

The boy cried when his father punished him.
父親處罰男孩時，他哭了出來。

puppy
[`pʌpɪ]
名 小狗

補充 chuckle 咯咯地笑
Our baby chuckles when he sees the puppy.
我們的小寶寶一看見小狗就笑了。

purple
[`pɝpḷ]
形 紫色的 名 紫色

補充 charming 迷人的
Olivia looks charming in that purple dress.
穿上紫色洋裝的奧莉維亞看起來很迷人。

purpose
[`pɝpəs]
名 目的

補充 on purpose 故意地
Adam broke his plate on purpose.
亞當故意打破他的盤子。

purse
[pɜs]
名 錢包

The man bought an expensive purse for his wife.
那位男士買了一個昂貴的錢包給他太太。

push
[puʃ]
動 名 推開

補充 push sb. away 把某人推開
The woman got mad when Leo pushed her away.
女人被里歐推開，因而憤怒不已。

put
[pʊt]
動 放置

補充 laptop 筆電
Carl put his laptop on the desk and went out.
卡爾把筆電放在桌上就出去了。

puzzle
[`pʌzl]
名 難題；謎 動 使迷惑

補充 crossword 填字謎遊戲
My father is trying to solve a crossword puzzle.
我爸爸正在試著解出一道填字遊戲。

Unit 17 Qq 字頭單字

MP3 17

quarter
[`kwɔrtɚ]
名 四分之一；美金25分；
十五分鐘

Nick drove 10 miles and a quarter to see his girlfriend.
尼克開了十又四分之一英里的車去見他女友。

queen
[kwin]
名 皇后；女王

補充 name after 以…的名字來命名
This avenue was named after Queen Elizabeth.
這條大道是按伊莉莎白女王的名字命名。

question
[`kwɛstʃən]
名 問題 動 質疑

補充 complicated 複雜的、難懂的
It's a simple question. Don't make it too complicated.
這只是一個簡單的問題，不要把它搞得太複雜。

quick
[kwɪk]
形 快的；迅速的

I had a quick coffee this morning because I am almost late.
由於早上快遲到，所以我快速地喝完咖啡。

quiet
[`kwaɪət]
形 安靜的

The children stayed quiet until the exam was over.
在考試結束之前，孩子們都保持安靜。

quit
[kwɪt]
動 放棄；離職

補充 fierce 激烈的 / argument 爭執
Dylan quit his job after the fierce argument with his boss.
在與上司的激烈爭吵後，狄倫辭掉了工作。

quite
[kwaɪt]
副 相當地

Louis was quite shy when he was little.
路易斯小時候相當害羞。

quiz
[kwɪz]
名 小考；測驗

The teacher gave us a quiz in English this afternoon.
老師今天下午對我們進行了英文測驗。

Unit 18 Rr 字頭單字

R.O.C. / ROC
縮 中華民國

補充 ROC = Republic of China
October 10th is the National Day of ROC.
十月十日是中華民國的國慶日。

rabbit
[`ræbɪt]
名 兔子

The hunter set traps to catch the rabbits.
獵人設下陷阱以獵捕兔子。

race
[res]
名 競賽；種族
動 與…賽跑

The runner broke the record for the half-mile race.
跑者打破了半英里賽跑的紀錄。

radio
[`redɪˌo]
名 收音機

No matter how many times I try, the radio still cannot work.
不管我試了幾次，收音機就是無法運轉。

railroad
[`relˌrod]
名 鐵路

This railroad connects two big cities.
這條鐵路連接兩個大城市。

railway
[`relˌwe]
名 鐵路

補充 barely 幾乎不 / fare（交通工具的）票價
We could barely afford the high-speed railway fare.
我們付不起高鐵車費。

rain
[ren]
名 雨 **動** 下雨

The plum rain season came early this year.
今年的梅雨季提早到來。

rainbow
[`ren, bo]
名 彩虹

補充 aborigine 原住民
The aborigines believed rainbow is a sign of God.
那些原住民相信彩虹是神明顯靈。

raincoat
[`ren, kot]
名 雨衣

The weather is cloudy, so he brings a raincoat with him.
天氣陰陰的,所以他隨身攜帶雨衣。

rainy
[`renɪ]
形 下雨的;多雨的

The old man waited outside in a cold and rainy day.
在這樣冷颼颼的雨天,老先生在外等候著。

raise
[rez]
動 舉起;提高

補充 mighty 強有力的 / blow 一擊
Danny raised the rock and struck the wall with a mighty blow.
丹尼舉起岩石,重重地砸在牆上。

rare
[rɛr]
形 罕見的;稀有的

The butterfly is a kind of rare species.
這種蝴蝶是稀有品種。

rat
[ræt]
名 老鼠

補充 指的是一般人害怕的大灰鼠
The rats snuggle together to keep warm in the cold weather.
這些老鼠在天冷時依偎在一起取暖。

rather
[`ræðɚ]
副 寧可;頗為

補充 would rather...than... 寧願(接原形動詞)
I would rather stay home than hang out with them.
與其和他們瞎混,我寧願待在家。

reach
[ritʃ]
動 到達;伸出

We've reached an agreement that is good for both sides.
我們達成了協議,這對雙方都有好處。

187

read
[rid]
動 閱讀

After reading his journal, Ann realized she had mistaken him.
讀了他的日記之後，安才發現錯怪他了。

ready
[`rɛdɪ]
形 準備好的

We are ready for our trip.
我們準備好啟程去旅行了。

real
[`riəl]
形 真實的；真正的

I don't think her diamond is real.
我認為她的鑽石是假的。

realize
[`riəlaɪz]
動 實現；認識到

補充 strive to 努力、奮鬥（後接動詞）
Steve strives to realize his dreams.
史蒂夫努力實現自己的夢想。

reason
[`rizṇ]
名 理由

Did you break up with your boyfriend for some reason?
你和男友分手有什麼原因嗎？

receive
[rɪ`siv]
動 收到

補充 master's degree 碩士學位
I recently received my master's degree in accounting.
我最近拿到會計的碩士文憑。

record
[`rɛkəd]
名 紀錄；唱片
動 記錄；錄音

補充 當動詞時，發音為 [rɪ`kɔrd]
Kathy kept her son's health record for later reference.
凱西保存她兒子的醫療紀錄，以便日後查詢。

recover
[rɪ`kʌvə]
動 恢復；尋回

She has not recovered from the shock of her son's death.
她還沒有從兒子逝世的打擊中恢復過來。

rectangle
[`rɛktæŋgḷ]
名 長方形

Tony folded the sheet into a neat rectangle.
東尼將床單摺成一個整齊的長方形。

recycle
[ri`saɪkḷ]
動 回收；再利用

補充 bundle 捆、把…紮成一包
I bundled all the magazines and recycled them.
我把雜誌捆成一團，並拿去資源回收。

red
[rɛd]
形 紅色的 名 紅色

The teacher asks us to correct our answers with a red pen.
老師要求我們用紅筆修正答案。

refrigerator
[rɪ`frɪdʒə͵retə]
名 電冰箱

補充 口語上更常用 fridge 稱呼
How much milk tea is there in the refrigerator?
冰箱裡有多少奶茶？

refuse
[rɪ`fjuz]
動 拒絕

The bank refused to give him another loan.
銀行拒絕再讓他貸款。

regret
[rɪ`grɛt]
動 懊悔；後悔

Come here immediately, or you will regret.
馬上過來這裡，否則你會後悔。

regular
[`rɛgjələ]
形 通常的；定期的

All the managers must attend the regular meetings.
所有經理都必須參加定期會議。

reject
[rɪ`dʒɛkt]
動 拒絕

The bank rejected our loan application.
銀行拒絕了我們的貸款申請。

relative
[`rɛlətɪv]
形 相關的 名 親戚

Are these documents relative to the issue?
這些文件與議題有關嗎？

remember
[rɪ`mɛmbə]
動 記得

I can't even remember when I last saw Daniel.
我甚至不記得我上一次看到丹尼爾是什麼時候的事了。

remind
[rɪ`maɪnd]
動 提醒

補充 tactic 戰術、策略
The coach shouted to remind his players of the tactics.
教練大喊著，提醒球員們戰術內容。

rent
[rɛnt]
動 租借 名 租金

補充 三態變化為 rent, rented, rented
The hut can be rented at a lower price during the off-season.
淡季時，小屋能以較低的價格出租。

repair
[rɪ`pɛr]
動 名 修理

It costs me three thousand dollars to repair my computer.
修電腦花了我三千美元。

repeat
[rɪ`pit]
動 名 重複

He was just repeating what Mr. Hill said.
他只是在重複希爾先生說的話。

report
[rɪ`port]
名 報告

Professor Lee asked Mark to rewrite his report.
李教授要求馬克重寫他的報告。

reporter
[rɪ`portə]
名 記者

補充 press conference 記者招待會
The reporter wondered why they cancel the press conference.
那名記者不明白他們為何取消記者會。

respect
[rɪˋspɛkt]
動 名 尊敬

I respect the firefighters for they've saved so many lives.
我很尊敬消防員，因為他們拯救了許多生命。

responsible
[rɪˋspɑnsəbḷ]
形 負責任的

Bill still felt responsible for her death until now.
直到現在，比爾仍覺得她的死是自己造成的。

rest
[rɛst]
動 名 休息

補充 take a rest 休息 / lounge 會客廳
I prefer to take a rest at the airport lounge.
我比較想要在機場大廳先休息一下。

restaurant
[ˋrɛstərənt]
名 餐廳

補充 reserve a table 訂位
You should have reserved a table at the restaurant earlier.
你應該更早一點向餐廳訂位的。

restroom
[ˋrɛst͵rum]
名 洗手間

I didn't go to the restroom because I was waiting for the interview.
因為在等待面試，所以我沒去洗手間。

result
[rɪˋzʌlt]
名 結果

Can we report the result to the manager?
我們能把結果報告給經理了嗎？

return
[rɪˋtɜn]
動 返回；歸還

補充 refill 再裝滿
You need to refill it before returning the car.
歸還車子前，你必須替它加滿油。

review
[rɪˋvju]
動 名 複習

I usually review my notes before an exam.
我通常會在考試前複習筆記。

revise
[rɪˋvaɪz]
動 校訂；更改

Two editors handled the work of revising the book.
兩位編輯處理這本書的校訂工作。

rice
[raɪs]
名 稻米；飯

補充 greasy 油膩的、多脂的
The fried rice is too salty and greasy.
這個炒飯太鹹又太油了。

rich
[rɪtʃ]
形 富有的

補充 show off 炫耀、賣弄
The rich woman likes to show off her jewels.
這名貴婦喜歡炫耀她的寶石。

ride
[raɪd]
動 騎；乘 名 搭乘

They used to ride horses on the track around the lake.
他們以前常繞著湖邊的路徑騎馬。

right
[raɪt]
形 右邊的；正確的
名 右邊；權利

補充 slide 滑動、滑落
Snow slides down from the right side of the mountain.
雪從山的右側滑落。

ring
[rɪŋ]
名 戒指；鈴聲 動 按鈴

補充 incredibly 難以置信地
The price of her wedding ring is incredibly high.
她結婚戒指的價格高得驚人。

rise
[raɪz]
動 上升 名 升起

The rent is going to rise next year.
租金明年起將調漲。

river
[ˋrɪvɚ]
名 河流

補充 prohibit 禁止 / due to 因為
Camping is prohibited by the river due to the pollution.
由於汙染問題，河邊禁止露營。

road
[rod]
名 道路

Perhaps it's a matter of age that I have difficulty seeing the road map.
也許是年齡問題吧，我看不清地圖。

rob
[rɑb]
動 搶劫

The woman was robbed this afternoon.
那名婦人今天下午被搶劫了。

robot
[`robət]
名 機器人

The scientist invented a new type of robot.
這名科學家發明了一種新型機器人。

rock
[rɑk]
名 岩石；搖滾樂 動 搖動

The kids were trying to find some pretty shells or rocks.
孩子們試著尋找漂亮的貝殼或石頭。

role
[rol]
名 角色

補充 significant 重大的、有意義的
Do you think that your friends play a significant role in your life?
朋友在你的生活中扮演很重要的角色嗎？

roll
[rol]
動 捲；滾

補充 sleeve 袖子
Zack rolled up his sleeves before he moved the boxes.
在搬箱子之前，查克捲起了袖子。

roof
[ruf]
名 屋頂

補充 leak 漏、滲
The roof is leaking after the heavy rain.
大雨過後，屋頂開始漏水了。

room
[rum]
名 房間

補充 living room 客廳
I want to rent an apartment with one bedroom and a living room.
我想租一房一廳的公寓。

root
[rut]
名 根;根源

補充 laziness 怠惰、懶散
Laziness is the root of all evil.
懶散是萬惡根源。

rope
[rop]
名 繩子

The robbers tied Danny up with a rope.
強盜用繩子把丹尼綁起來。

round
[raʊnd]
形 圓形的

補充 medium 中等的 / length 長度
I've got a round face and medium-length, black hair.
我有一張圓臉蛋,以及黑色的中長髮。

row
[ro]
動 划船 名 一排;一列

People rowed together on Dragon Boat Festival.
人們在端午節一起划龍舟。

rub
[rʌb]
動 磨擦

You should rub your hands with soap.
你應該在手上抹些肥皂。

rubber
[`rʌbɚ]
名 橡膠

These two pairs of gloves are made of rubber.
這兩雙手套是用橡膠做的。

rude
[rud]
形 粗魯的;無禮的

It is rude to talk on your phone while watching movies.
邊看電影邊講電話是很失禮的行為。

ruin
[`ruɪn]
動 毀滅;破壞

She blamed Adam for he has ruined everything.
她責怪亞當破壞了一切。

rule
[rul]
名 規則 動 統治

Tracy has no idea about the rules of soccer.
崔西完全不懂足球的規則。

ruler
[`rulɚ]
名 尺;統治者

You should use a ruler to draw the line.
你應該用一把尺來畫這條線。

run
[rʌn]
動 跑;經營

補充 toothpaste 牙膏
I'll wait in line and you can run to get the toothpaste.
我來排隊,這樣你就能跑去拿牙膏。

rush
[rʌʃ]
動 催促;急送

補充 strike(鐘)敲響報時
When it struck twelve, all the workers rushed to the restaurant.
當時鐘敲響十二點,所有工人都衝往餐廳。

Unit
19
Ss 字頭單字

MP3 19

sad
[sæd]
形 難過的

When he heard the sad news, he could not stop weeping.
聽到這令人難過的消息時,他忍不住流淚。

safe
[sef]
形 安全的

補充 snorkel 浮潛
How about going snorkeling? It's safe and fun.
去浮潛怎麼樣?安全又有趣。

safety
[`seftɪ]
名 安全

Mr. and Mrs. Smith only care about their son's safety.
史密斯夫婦只關心他們兒子的安全。

sail
[sel]
動 航行

Billy's dream is to sail around the world.
比利的夢想是航海環遊世界。

sailor
[`selɚ]
名 水手；船員

補充 frequently 頻繁地、屢次地
Sailors cannot go home frequently.
船員們無法時常回家。

salad
[`sæləd]
名 沙拉

補充 olive 橄欖 / mustard 芥末
I use garlic, olive oil, mustard and cheese to make salad dressing.
我用大蒜、橄欖油、芥末與起司來製作沙拉醬。

sale
[sel]
名 賣；出售

補充 on sale 上市的、出售的
All the items in the store are on sale now.
現在這家店裡的所有物品都在拍賣。

salesman
[`selzmən]
名 銷售員；業務員

My secretary canceled my interview with the salesman.
我祕書取消了我和那名業務員的會面。

salt
[sɔlt]
名 鹽

You'd better not take so much salt and sugar.
你最好別攝取那麼多鹽分與糖分。

same
[sem]
形 同樣的

Tony promised that he won't make the same mistake again.
東尼承諾他不會再犯同樣的錯誤。

sample
[`sæmpl]
名 樣品；樣本

The customer asked for a sample of the new product.
那位顧客要求拿一個新產品的樣本。

sand
[sænd]
名 沙子

I hate walking on the hot sand at the beach.
我討厭走在海邊又熱又燙的沙子上。

sandwich
[`sændwɪtʃ]
名 三明治

He ordered a chicken sandwich and a large order of French fries.
他點了一份雞肉三明治與大份薯條。

satisfy
[`sætɪs‚faɪ]
動 使滿足

Joe satisfied his daughter by taking her to the zoo.
喬帶女兒去動物園玩，好讓她開心。

Saturday
[`sætə‚de]
名 星期六

Saturday night is our busiest night of the week.
週六晚上是我們整個星期最忙的時段。

saucer
[`sɔsə]
名 淺碟

My aunt loves buying beautiful sets of cups and saucers.
我阿姨很喜歡買漂亮的杯碟組。

save
[sev]
動 儲蓄；節省；救

Sending letters by express mail saves a lot of time.
用快遞寄信能省下很多時間。

say
[se]
動 說

補充 discharge 允許…出院
The doctor said I can be discharged tomorrow morning.
醫生說我明天早上就能出院了。

scared
[skɛrd]
形 害怕的

Lydia felt scared and then sit closer to us.
莉蒂亞感到害怕，因而往我們這邊挪動座位。

scarf
[skɑrf]
名 圍巾

補充 drop（價格、溫度等）下降
She wore a scarf because the temperature dropped.
由於氣溫下降，她戴了一條圍巾。

scene
[sin]
名 場面；景色

補充 terrific 嚇人的、（口）非常好的
This is the most terrific scene I have ever seen.
這是我看過最恐怖的場景。

scenery
[`sinərɪ]
名 風景；景色

補充 surround 圍繞 / campsite 露營地
We loved the scenery surrounding the campsite.
我們喜愛露營地四周的風景。

school
[skul]
名 學校

Kelly went to graduate school in the States three years ago.
凱莉三年前到美國唸研究所。

science
[`saɪəns]
名 科學

The little boy showed great interest in science.
小男孩顯露出他對科學的高度興趣。

scientist
[`saɪəntɪst]
名 科學家

補充 inhabitant 居民
The scientist warned the inhabitants not to drink the polluted water.
科學家警告居民不要喝被汙染的水。

scooter
[`skutɚ]
名 機車

補充 指座位前方有腳踏平台的機車
Tim rides his scooter to work every day.
提姆每天騎機車上班。

score
[skor]
名 分數;樂譜 動 得分

Lisa studied very hard to earn a high score on TOEFL.
為了在托福測驗中獲得高分,麗莎非常努力唸書。

screen
[skrin]
名 螢光幕 動 放映;篩選

補充 scratch 刮痕、抓痕
I need to buy a screen protector to avoid scratches.
我必須買螢幕保護貼,以防刮痕。

sea
[si]
名 海洋

Most of the earth's surface is covered by sea.
地球表面大部分都被海洋所覆蓋。

seafood
[`si.fud]
名 海產;海鮮

補充 pasta 義大利麵 / scallop 扇貝
To make seafood pasta, we need to buy some shrimp and scallops.
為了做海鮮義大利麵,我們得先買蝦子和貝類。

search
[sɝtʃ]
動 搜尋;搜查

補充 online 連線地,此處為副詞
You can search travel information online.
你可以上網搜尋旅遊資訊。

season
[`sizn̩]
名 季節

I like cool and windy days, so autumn is my favorite season.
我喜歡涼爽有風的天氣,所以秋天是我最愛的季節。

seat
[sit]
名 座位

Excuse me. Is this seat taken?
不好意思,請問這個位子有人坐了嗎?

second
[`sɛkənd]
形 第二的 名 第二;秒

The financial and accounting departments are on the second floor.
財務與會計部門位於二樓。

secondary
[`sɛkən,dɛrɪ]
形 第二的；次要的

Prime advice is important, but we also need secondary ones.
主要意見很重要，但我們也需要次要意見。

secret
[`sikrɪt]
名 祕密

Don't try to tell her any secret between us.
別告訴她我們之間的祕密。

secretary
[`sɛkrə,tɛrɪ]
名 祕書

Tracy has been a secretary for eight years.
崔西當了八年的祕書。

section
[`sɛkʃən]
名 部分；片；塊

I haven't read the last two sections of this novel.
我還沒有閱讀這本小說的最後兩個章節。

see
[si]
動 看見

補充 三態變化為 see, saw, seen
I called Jason when I saw his resume on the Internet.
在網路上看到傑森的履歷時，我便打電話給他。

seed
[sid]
名 種子

補充 hatred 憎恨 / battle 戰鬥
Hatred is the seed of battle.
憎恨是戰爭的種子。

seek
[sik]
動 尋覓

When you are seeking an apartment, the neighborhood is very important.
找公寓時，鄰近環境非常重要。

seem
[sim]
動 似乎是

There seems to be something wrong with my car.
我的車子似乎出了點問題。

seesaw
[`si,sɔ]
名 蹺蹺板

They used to play on the seesaw in the playground.
他們以前常在遊樂場裡玩蹺蹺板。

seldom
[`sɛldəm]
副 很少地；不常

We seldom hang out. We usually chat on the phone.
我們很少一起出去玩，通常都是講電話而已。

select
[sə`lɛkt]
動 挑選

Laura selected blue fabric for her new dress.
蘿拉挑了藍色布料做她的新洋裝。

selfish
[`sɛlfɪʃ]
形 自私的

Nobody wants to be Tom's friend because he's so selfish.
沒有人想跟湯姆做朋友，因為他太自私了。

sell
[sɛl]
動 賣

補充 be sold out 售罄
All tickets for the concert have been sold out.
這場音樂會的票都賣光了。

semester
[sə`mɛstə]
名 學期

補充 sophomore 二年級生 / junior 三年級生
I am a sophomore now and will be a junior next semester.
我現在大二，下學期就是大三生了。

send
[sɛnd]
動 寄；發送

I want to send this letter to America. How long does it take?
我想寄信到美國，請問需要多久時間呢？

senior high school
片 高級中學

I am getting used to the life of being a senior high school student.
我已漸漸適應高中生活。

sense
[sɛns]
名 感官；感覺

Jenny has no sense of direction.
珍妮毫無方向感。

sentence
[`sɛntəns]
名 句子 動 宣判；判決

Brian underlines the sentences he likes.
布萊恩在他喜歡的句子底下畫線。

September
[sɛp`tɛmbɚ]
名 九月

Our wedding anniversary is on September 10th.
我們的結婚週年紀念日是九月十日。

serious
[`sɪrɪəs]
形 嚴肅的；嚴重的；認真的

I have never had such a serious stomachache before.
我以前從沒胃痛得這麼厲害。

servant
[`sɝvənt]
名 僕人

補充 public servant 公僕；公務員
My uncle is a public servant who works for the government.
我舅舅是為政府工作的公務員。

serve
[sɝv]
動 為…服務；招待

We serve the best roast beef sandwich and onion rings.
我們提供最美味的烤牛肉三明治和洋蔥圈。

service
[`sɝvɪs]
名 服務

補充 transfer 轉接、轉換
Nina picked up the phone and transferred it to customer service.
妮娜接起電話，並轉接給客服。

set
[sɛt]
動 設定；安放
名 一套；一組

I'd like to set the meeting schedule as soon as possible.
我希望能盡快安排會議的時間。

seven
[`sɛvən]
形 七的 名 七

This new laptop comes in seven different colors to choose from.
這款新筆電推出了七種顏色可選。

seventeen
[,sɛvən`tin]
形 十七的 名 十七

補充 例句中的 story/stories 指「樓層」
The building we live in is seventeen stories high.
我們住的這棟建築物有十七層樓高。

seventy
[`sɛvəntɪ]
形 七十的 名 七十

補充 leather 皮革的 / window 商店櫥窗
The leather purse in the window is seventy US dollars.
櫥窗內的皮包售價七十美元。

several
[`sɛvərəl]
形 幾個的

補充 ruins 廢墟 / monument 紀念碑
We visited the ruins of a castle and several ancient monuments.
我們參觀了一座城堡遺跡和幾個古代紀念碑。

shake
[ʃek]
動 名 搖動

補充 panic 感到驚慌、使恐慌
Everyone panicked because the whole building was shaking.
整棟建築物都在搖晃，令大家驚恐不已。

shall
[ʃæl]
助 將；應該

What shall we cook tonight for the party?
我們該為今天晚上的派對煮些什麼呢？

shape
[ʃep]
名 形狀

補充 work out 健身
Tony stays in shape by working out.
東尼靠健身來維持身材。

share
[ʃɛr]
動 分享

My sister and I shared a room when we were kids.
小時候，我姐姐和我同睡一間房。

shark
[ʃɑrk]
名 鯊魚

補充 charge at 衝鋒、向前衝
The shark charged at those little fish.
鯊魚朝著那些小魚衝去。

sharp
[ʃɑrp]
形 尖銳的；敏銳的

補充 blade 刀身、刀片
The blade of the knife is sharp, so be careful.
這把刀子的刀鋒很利，請小心。

she
[ʃi]
代 她

補充 her 她（受格）、她的 / hers 她的東西
She always knows what hairstyles are in.
她總是很清楚時下最流行的髮型是什麼。

sheep
[ʃip]
名 綿羊

補充 sheep 的單複數同形，皆為 sheep
The man bought three heads of sheep from the farmer.
男子向農夫買進三頭羊。

sheet
[ʃit]
名 一張（紙）；床單

I helped my mother change her bed sheet yesterday.
我昨天幫忙母親更換她的床單。

shelf
[ʃɛlf]
名 架子

That author's novels are on the top shelf.
那名作者的小說放在最上面的架上。

shine
[ʃaɪn]
動 照耀；發光

補充 三態變化為 shine, shone, shone
The weather is great today. The sun shines in splendor.
今天天氣很好，陽光十分燦爛。

ship
[ʃɪp]
名 船 動 運送

補充 wreck 遇難
The ship was wrecked in the hurricane.
這艘船因暴風雨而發生船難。

shirt
[ʃɝt]
名 襯衫

補充 striped 條紋的（KK 為 [straɪpt]）
Thomas liked the striped shirt in the window.
湯瑪斯喜歡櫥窗裡的那件條紋襯衫。

shoe
[ʃu]
名 鞋子

He was looking for a pair of shoes for a formal dinner party.
他在找適合正式晚宴中穿的鞋子。

shoot
[ʃut]
動 射擊；注射；拍攝

補充 kidnapper 綁票者
A kidnapper was shot dead by the police.
一名綁匪被警方擊斃。

shop
[ʃɑp]
名 商店 動 購物

Janet worked in a fashion shop last winter.
珍妮特去年冬天在一間時尚店工作。

shopkeeper
[`ʃɑp͵kipɚ]
名 店主

補充 at times 有時、不時
The shopkeeper is nice and gives me free samples at times.
店主人很好，時不時會送我一些免費樣品。

shore
[ʃor]
名 岸邊

補充 a school of 一群（魚或海洋生物）
We saw a school of dolphins near the shore.
我們在海岸附近看到一群海豚。

short
[ʃɔrt]
形 矮的；短的

My nephew is a bit too short for his age.
我姪子在他那個年齡當中，顯得太矮了。

shorts
[ʃɔrts]
名 短褲

Why don't you wear shorts more often?
你為何不多穿短褲呢？

should
[ʃʊd]
助 應該；竟然

補充 sweep 掃 / dust 除去灰塵
Sweeping or dusting should be done on New Year's Day.
新年那天必須徹底打掃乾淨。

shoulder
[`ʃoldə]
名 肩膀

She looks gorgeous with shoulder-length hair.
及肩長髮讓她看起來棒極了。

shout
[ʃaʊt]
動 喊叫；呼喊

Those two men were shouting to each other.
那兩個男人對著彼此吼叫。

show
[ʃo]
動 出示；顯示 名 展覽

The engineer showed us how to use the machine.
工程師展示機器的使用方法給我們看。

shower
[`ʃaʊə]
動 名 淋浴

補充 take a shower 淋浴
You can use the shower room whenever you like.
你想什麼時候使用淋浴間都可以。

shrimp
[ʃrɪmp]
名 蝦子

The cook removed the heads and shells from the shrimp.
廚師摘除了蝦子的頭和殼。

shut
[ʃʌt]
動 關閉；閉上

補充 三態變化為 shut, shut, shut
Please shut the door when you leave.
離開的時候請關上門。

shy
[ʃaɪ]
形 害羞的

Jerry was too shy to express his feelings.
傑瑞太害羞了，無法好好表達他的感受。

sick
[sɪk]
形 生病的

I still feel sick after taking some over-the-counter medicine.
即使服用了成藥，我還是覺得不舒服。

---

side
[saɪd]
名 邊；面；旁邊

補充 side effects 副作用
Lisa is an optimistic person who always looks on the bright side.
麗莎生性樂觀，看事物總看向光明的一面。

---

sidewalk
[`saɪd.wɔk]
名 人行道

補充 briskly 輕快地、活潑地
Peter walked briskly along the sidewalk.
彼得輕快地沿著這條人行道往前走。

---

sight
[saɪt]
名 視力；見解

The old woman got sick and lost her sight.
老婦人染病且失明了。

---

sign
[saɪn]
動 簽署 名 記號

Are you ready to sign the contract?
你準備好要簽約了嗎？

---

silence
[`saɪləns]
名 寂靜；沉默

None of us break the silence between Joan and Bill.
我們當中沒有人打破瓊安和比爾之間的沉默。

---

silent
[`saɪlənt]
形 寂靜的；沉默的

補充 switch 改變、轉移
We didn't hear the ring because he switched it to silent mode.
他轉到靜音模式，所以我們沒聽到鈴聲。

---

silly
[`sɪlɪ]
形 傻的

補充 make up 編造、補足
It is silly to make up a story like that.
編造出那樣的故事是很愚蠢的一件事。

silver
[`sɪlvɚ]
形 銀製的;銀色的 名 銀

My cousin only wears plain silver necklaces and earrings.
我堂姊只戴純銀項鍊和耳環。

similar
[`sɪmələ]
形 相似的

It's easier to become friends if two people have similar backgrounds.
兩個人的成長背景相似,就比較容易成為朋友。

simple
[`sɪmpl̩]
形 簡單的

Don't worry. Let me show you some simple steps.
別擔心,讓我來教你一些簡單的步驟。

since
[sɪns]
連 自從;因為 介 自從

補充 nearsighted 近視眼的
Wendy has been nearsighted since she was a kid.
溫蒂從小就近視。

sincere
[sɪn`sɪr]
形 誠懇的;誠摯的

Rick was attracted by her direct and sincere personality.
瑞克被她率直又誠懇的性格所吸引。

sing
[sɪŋ]
動 唱歌

補充 三態變化為 sing, sang, sung
He walked in when the chorus was singing "Amazing Grace".
合唱團演唱《奇異恩典》時他走了進來。

singer
[`sɪŋɚ]
名 歌手

Ariana Grande is considered to be a natural singer.
亞莉安娜·格蘭德被視為一名天生的歌手。

single
[`sɪŋgl̩]
形 單一的;單身的
名 單身者

補充 bring up 養育、教育
Karen is a single mother who brought up her son by herself.
凱倫是單親媽媽,她獨自將兒子拉拔長大。

sink
[sɪŋk]
動 沉入;陷於 名 水槽

Hold your nose and sink yourself in the water.
捏住你的鼻子再沉入水中。

sir
[sɝ]
名 先生

Sir, I am afraid you are at the wrong counter.
先生,您恐怕找錯櫃檯了。

sister
[`sɪstɚ]
名 姐姐;妹妹

補充 bridesmaid 伴娘 / best man 伴郎
My younger sister would be my bridesmaid.
我妹妹會擔任我的伴娘。

sit
[sɪt]
動 坐下

I don't like to sit close to the band. It's too loud.
我不喜歡坐得太靠近樂團,太吵了。

six
[sɪks]
形 六的 名 六

補充 dye 染色 / perm 燙髮
My mother has her hair dyed and permed every six months.
我媽媽每六個月就會去染髮和燙髮。

sixteen
[ˌsɪks`tin]
形 十六的 名 十六

Penny lost about sixteen pounds in two months.
佩妮在兩個月內瘦了大約十六磅。

sixty
[`sɪkstɪ]
形 六十的 名 六十

I only got sixty points on the math test.
我數學只考了六十分。

size
[saɪz]
名 大小;尺寸

We would like a double room with a king size bed.
我們想要訂一間附特大雙人床的雙人房。

skate
[sket]
動 溜冰 名 溜冰鞋

My ten-year-old niece is skating a figure of eight.
我十歲的姪女正在溜八字形。

ski
[ski]
動 滑雪 名 滑雪板

Ian goes skiing in Korea every winter.
伊恩每年冬天都去韓國滑雪。

skill
[skɪl]
名 技能

補充 communication 溝通 / ability 能力
He has good communication skills and problem-solving abilities.
他擁有優秀的溝通技巧與解決問題的能力。

skillful
[`skɪlfəl]
形 熟練的；靈巧的

補充 negotiator 交涉者、談判者
We need a skillful negotiator.
我們需要一名技巧熟練的協商人員。

skin
[skɪn]
名 皮膚

補充 rash 疹子 / cosmetics 化妝品
Dora has a skin rash caused by cosmetics.
化妝品是造成朵拉皮膚起疹子的原因。

skinny
[`skɪnɪ]
形 很瘦的；皮包骨的

Look at those poor kids. How skinny they are!
看看那些可憐的孩子們，都瘦成皮包骨了！

skirt
[skɜt]
名 裙子

I think this kind of skirt will stay in fashion for a few more years.
我覺得這種裙子還會再流行個幾年。

sky
[skaɪ]
名 天空

The artist finished his painting with a few last touches on the sky.
畫家在天空畫了最後幾筆，完成他的畫作。

sleep
[slip]
動 睡覺 **名** 睡眠

Danny went to the doctor because he has trouble sleeping.
丹尼有睡不好的困擾，所以他去看醫生。

sleepy
[`slipɪ]
形 想睡的

補充 pinch 捏、擰 / thigh 大腿
He pinched his thigh when he felt sleepy in class.
上課想睡時，他就捏自己的大腿。

slender
[`slɛndə]
形 苗條的；纖細的

Heidi is beautiful and slender. We all want to be like her.
海蒂既漂亮又苗條，我們都想像她一樣。

slice
[slaɪs]
名 薄片 **動** 切成薄片

Why don't we buy a couple slices of ham for breakfast?
我們為何不買幾片火腿來做早餐？

slide
[slaɪd]
動 滑動 **名** 下滑

補充 動詞三態變化為 slide, slid, slid
The car slid on the slope.
車子在斜坡上滑動。

slim
[slɪm]
形 苗條的；微薄的

Jennifer is a slim woman with long hair.
珍妮佛是一位身材苗條、留長髮的女性。

slipper
[`slɪpə]
名 拖鞋

補充 strike, struck, struck 打、攻擊
My father struck the cockroach with a slipper.
我爸爸用拖鞋打蟑螂。

slow
[slo]
形 緩慢的 **動** 使慢下來

補充 slow down 慢下來、減慢速度
Life is easy and slow in this small island.
這座小島上的生活很安逸，步調也緩慢。

small
[smɔl]
形 小的

補充 delicate 精美的
Small and delicate earrings are great gifts for Lucy.
小而精巧的耳環對露西來說是很棒的禮物。

smart
[smɑrt]
形 聰明的

I like Gloria because she is very smart and considerate.
我喜歡葛洛莉雅，她非常聰明又體貼。

smell
[smɛl]
動 聞到 名 氣味

What's in the pot? I smell something burning.
鍋子裡有什麼？我聞到燒焦的味道了。

smile
[smaɪl]
名 動 微笑

Lily always wears a smile when she talks to others.
與別人交談時，莉莉總是帶著笑容。

smoke
[smok]
動 抽菸；冒煙 名 煙

I saw Johnny smoking near the parking lot.
我看到強尼在停車場附近抽菸。

snack
[snæk]
名 點心

Do you eat popcorn or other snacks while watching a movie?
你看電影的時候會吃爆米花或其他點心嗎？

snail
[snel]
名 蝸牛

The little girl drew a picture of a snail.
小女孩畫了一隻蝸牛。

snake
[snek]
名 蛇

補充 crawl 爬行、蠕動
I saw a snake crawling into your sleeping bag.
我看到一條蛇爬進你的睡袋。

sneaker
[ˋsnikɚ]
名 球鞋；運動鞋

My parents gave me sneakers for Christmas.
我的父母送我運動鞋作為聖誕禮物。

sneaky
[ˋsnikɪ]
形 鬼鬼祟祟的

補充 peep 窺、偷看
Did you see a sneaky guy peeping from the front yard?
你有看見一名行跡鬼祟的男子在前院偷窺嗎？

snow
[sno]
名 雪 動 下雪

The kids went outside to see the first snow of this winter.
孩子們跑出去看今年冬天的第一場雪。

snowman
[ˋsno͵mæn]
名 雪人

We can make a snowman if the snow is heavy enough.
如果雪下得夠多，我們就能做雪人了。

snowy
[ˋsnoɪ]
形 多雪的；似雪的

Uncle Bill doesn't like the snowy weather.
比爾叔叔不喜歡多雪的天氣。

so
[so]
連 所以 副 如此地

We're running late, so I'd like to move on to the main points.
我們有點延誤了，所以我想直接進入正題。

soap
[sop]
名 肥皂

補充 souvenir 紀念品
Tracy bought a bar of soap as a souvenir.
崔西買了一塊肥皂作為紀念品。

soccer
[ˋsɑkɚ]
名 足球

Soccer is not a popular sport in Taiwan.
足球在臺灣並不流行。

213

social
[`soʃəl]
形 社會的；交際的

補充 demand 要求
There is a strong demand to solve social problems.
民眾強烈要求解決社會問題。

society
[sə`saɪətɪ]
名 社會

補充 aboriginal 原住民 / minority 少數
The aboriginals are the minority in our society.
原住民為我們社會的少數族群。

sock
[sɑk]
名 襪子；短襪

補充 nylon 尼龍 / silk 絲的
Cotton socks are better than nylon or silk ones.
棉襪比尼龍或絲質的好。

soda
[`sodə]
名 汽水

Drinking too much soda is bad for your teeth.
喝太多汽水對你的牙齒不好。

sofa
[`sofə]
名 沙發

補充 cushion 墊子、坐墊
Where did you get the sofa and cushions?
你的沙發和墊子是在哪裡買的呢？

soft drink
片 不含酒精的飲料

補充 banquet 宴會、盛宴
Only soft drinks are offered in this banquet.
這場盛宴只提供無酒精飲料。

softball
[`sɔft͵bɔl]
名 壘球

My brother used to play softball with his friends.
我哥哥以前會和朋友一起打壘球。

soldier
[`soldʒɚ]
名 軍人；士兵

補充 weapon 武器、兵器
The soldiers were carrying weapons.
士兵們攜帶武器。

solve
[sɑlv]
動 解決

He could not solve the problem without your help.
沒有你的幫忙，他無法解決問題。

some
[sʌm]
形 一些的 代 一些

I have to take a day off tomorrow due to some personal stuff.
由於一些個人因素，我明天必須請假一天。

someone
[`sʌm, wʌn]
代 某人

補充 同義詞有 somebody
We need someone to fill that position.
我們需要找個人來補這個空缺。

something
[`sʌmθɪŋ]
代 某事

補充 brake 煞車（通常用複數形）
It seems that something is wrong with my brakes.
看起來我的煞車似乎有點問題。

sometimes
[`sʌm, taɪmz]
副 有時候

I sometimes go to clubs to listen to live music with friends.
我有時候會和朋友一起去酒吧聽現場演奏。

somewhere
[`sʌm, hwɛr]
副 在某處

Could we sit somewhere else, please?
請問我們能坐在別的地方嗎？

son
[sʌn]
名 兒子

補充 spill 使溢出、使濺出
I'm sorry that my son spilled the juice all over the table.
真的很抱歉，我兒子把果汁灑了滿桌。

song
[sɔŋ]
名 歌曲

補充 lyrics 歌詞（通常用複數形）
The lyrics of his latest song really touched me.
他新歌裡面的歌詞很觸動我。

215

soon
[sun]
副 很快地;不久

as soon as 一···就···
I will start looking for a job as soon as I graduate.
我一畢業就會開始找工作。

sore
[sor]
形 疼痛的

have a sore throat 喉嚨痛
I have a sore throat, so I took some medicine.
我喉嚨痛,所以吃了一些藥。

sorry
[`sɔrɪ]
形 抱歉的 感 對不起

Kevin is sorry for being careless.
凱文為自己的疏忽感到抱歉。

soul
[sol]
名 靈魂

All of us hope his soul will rest in peace.
我們都希望他的靈魂能得到安息。

sound
[saʊnd]
動 聽起來 名 聲音

That sounds more like what I had in mind.
那聽起來和我原本的構想比較相似。

soup
[sup]
名 湯

My mother makes the best pumpkin soup in the world.
我媽媽煮的南瓜湯是全世界最好喝的。

sour
[`saʊr]
形 酸的

We went to a Thai restaurant because the client likes spicy and sour food.
由於客戶喜歡又酸又辣的食物,所以我們去了泰式餐館。

south
[saʊθ]
形 南方的 副 向南 名 南方

The game will decide if South Korea reaches the Round of 8.
這場比賽攸關南韓能否晉級八強。

216

soy sauce
片 醬油

Soy sauce and vinegar are on my shopping list.
醬油和醋都在我的購物清單上。

space
[spes]
名 空間;宇宙

補充 plenty of 大量的
The hard drive surely has plenty of available space.
硬碟確實有足夠的空間可用。

spaghetti
[spə`gɛtɪ]
名 義大利麵

Karen is going to make spaghetti with meatballs.
凱倫要做肉丸義大利麵。

speak
[spik]
動 說;講

補充 三態為 speak, spoke, spoken
Adam can speak five foreign languages.
亞當會講五種外語。

speaker
[`spikɚ]
名 演講者;說話者

The speaker tonight is a famous American writer.
今晚的演講者是一位美國知名作家。

special
[`spɛʃəl]
形 特別的

Do you have any special plans for the weekend?
你週末有什麼特別的安排嗎?

speech
[spitʃ]
名 言論;演講

補充 impress 給…極深的印象
They were impressed by the scientist's speech.
他們都對那名科學家的演說印象深刻。

speed
[spid]
名 速度

Be careful with the speed limit when driving on highway.
行駛高速公路時要注意速限。

spell
[spɛl]
動 用字母拼

The little girl is trying to spell her name.
小女孩正試著拼出她的名字。

spend
[spɛnd]
動 花費（錢或時間）

How long do you spend surfing on the Internet every day?
你每天花在瀏覽網路上的時間有多久？

spider
[`spaɪdə]
名 蜘蛛

補充 spin, spun, spun 蜘蛛結網
I saw a spider spinning its web in a corner of the ceiling.
我看到一隻蜘蛛在天花板的角落結網。

spirit
[`spɪrɪt]
名 精神

That's the spirit we are looking for.
那就是我們所追求的精神。

spoon
[spun]
名 湯匙

補充 colleague 同事 / stir 攪拌
My colleague stirred his coffee with a spoon.
我同事用一支湯匙攪拌他的咖啡。

sport
[sport]
名 運動

We have a well-equipped sports center and two tennis courts.
我們有設施完善的運動中心和兩座網球場。

spot
[spɑt]
名 斑點；場所 **動** 注意到

Those red and yellow spots make the painting more colorful.
那些紅色與黃色的點點讓這幅畫更加生動。

spread
[sprɛd]
動 散布；擴散

補充 warn 警告 / rumor 謠言
Jason warned them to stop spreading the rumor.
傑森警告他們停止散布謠言。

spring
[sprɪŋ]
名 春天;泉

補充 hot spring 溫泉
Jenny and David's wedding will be held in spring.
珍妮與大衛的婚禮將在春天舉行。

square
[skwɛr]
形 正方形的 名 正方形

The four angles of a square are 90 degrees.
正方型的四個角都是九十度。

stair
[stɛr]
名 樓梯

補充 a flight of stairs 一段樓梯
The landlord walked up a flight of stairs to knock on his door.
房東走上一段樓梯去敲他的門。

stamp
[stæmp]
名 郵票 動 蓋印

I used to collect stamps when I was a kid, but I don't do it anymore.
我小時候曾集郵,但現在沒有了。

stand
[stænd]
動 站立;堅持
名 攤子;架子

補充 balance 保持平衡
The coach asked us to stand and balance on one leg.
教練要求我們用單腳站立,並保持平衡。

star
[stɑr]
名 星星;明星 動 主演

補充 twinkle 閃爍、閃耀
The stars are twinkling in the dark night.
星星在暗夜中閃爍。

start
[stɑrt]
動 名 開始

The parade will start at 6 p.m., followed by a fireworks show.
遊行將於傍晚六點開始,之後會有煙火秀。

state
[stet]
名 狀態;州 動 陳述

補充 名詞的其中一個用法為美國的州
Daniel is in a happy state these days.
丹尼爾最近心情很好。

station
[`steʃən]
名 車站

Many students work at gas stations and fast food restaurants.
很多學生會去加油站和速食店工作。

stationery
[`steʃən,ɛrɪ]
名 文具

補充 a variety of 各種各樣的
The stationery shop offers a variety of office supplies.
文具店裡販售各式各樣的辦公室用品。

stay
[ste]
動 名 停留

Where will you be staying during your trip?
你旅遊期間會住在哪裡？

steak
[stek]
名 牛排

Steak tastes the best when it is cooked medium.
五分熟的牛排是最好吃的。

steal
[stil]
動 偷竊

補充 motive 動機 / unknown 未知的
The motive of his stealing is still unknown.
他行竊的動機仍未釐清。

steam
[stim]
動 蒸 名 蒸氣

The fish is very fresh, so I made steamed fish.
魚很新鮮，所以我做了蒸魚。

step
[stɛp]
名 腳步 動 踏

補充 waltz 華爾滋舞
What are the basic steps for dancing a waltz?
華爾滋的基本舞步怎麼跳呢？

still
[stɪl]
副 仍然 形 靜止的

補充 duty-free 免稅的
We still have time for shopping at duty-free shops.
我們仍有時間去免稅店逛逛。

stingy
[`stɪndʒɪ]
形 吝嗇的；小氣的

The stingy man is the joke in our neighborhood.
那個吝嗇的男人是我們社區的笑柄。

stomach
[`stʌmək]
名 胃

I have had some stomach problems since I was a kid.
我從小胃就不是很好，有些問題。

stomachache
[`stʌmək‚ek]
名 胃痛

The actor got a bad stomachache before the show.
在演出之前，那名演員的胃痛得很厲害。

stone
[ston]
名 石頭

They climbed up the stone steps to the top of the hill.
他們爬上石階，抵達山頂。

stop
[stɑp]
動 停止；阻止

Joe and Lily stopped talking to each other for a month.
喬和莉莉已經一個月沒和彼此說話了。

store
[stor]
名 商店

補充 convenience store 便利商店
The department store is having an annual sale.
那間百貨公司在舉行週年慶。

storm
[stɔrm]
名 暴風雨 動 猛攻

補充 hut 小屋 / furious 狂暴的
The hut on the island was destroyed by a furious storm.
島上的小屋被暴風雨摧毀。

stormy
[`stɔrmɪ]
形 暴風雨的

Our ship went through the stormy seas safely.
我們的船平安通過暴風雨海面。

story
[`storɪ]
名 故事；樓層

Listening to scary stories gives me goosebumps.
聽鬼故事讓我起雞皮疙瘩。

stove
[stov]
名 爐子

補充 pot 鍋子 / heat 加熱
The pot is heated on the gas stove.
鍋子正放在瓦斯爐上加熱。

straight
[stret]
形 直的；坦率的

Nancy has long, straight hair and big eyes.
南西留著直長髮，還有一雙大眼睛。

strange
[strendʒ]
形 奇怪的

Patrick looked strange in those baggy pants.
穿著垮褲的派翠克看起來滿奇怪的。

straw
[strɔ]
名 稻草；吸管

Those campers made a fire with dry straws.
那幾名露營者用乾稻草生火。

strawberry
[`strɔbɛrɪ]
名 草莓

補充 freeze 結冰、凝住
Freezing the strawberries is a good way to keep them fresh.
把草莓冷凍起來是保持新鮮度的一個好辦法。

stream
[strim]
名 溪流 動 流動

There is a beautiful stream behind my house.
我家後面有一條很美的溪流。

street
[strit]
名 街道

We seldom shop in the supermarket across the street.
我們很少在對街的超市購物。

strike
[straɪk]
動 打擊 名 攻擊；罷工

補充 三態變化為 strike, struck, struck
The office building was struck by lightning.
那棟辦公大樓被閃電擊中。

string
[strɪŋ]
名 細繩；弦 動 連成一串

補充 gorgeous 華麗的
The string of pearls looks gorgeous on Ms. Hill.
那串珍珠戴在希爾小姐身上很美。

strong
[strɔŋ]
形 強壯的

Typhoons usually come with strong wind and heavy rain.
颱風通常都伴隨著強風與豪雨。

student
[`stjudn̩t]
名 學生

The play was written by a team of four students.
這個劇本是由四位學生合力寫成的。

study
[`stʌdɪ]
動 名 學習

Vivian stayed up all night studying because of the mid-term exam.
由於期中考，薇薇安熬夜了一整晚唸書。

stupid
[`stjupɪd]
形 笨的

It was stupid for him to buy the vase at such a high price.
他用這麼高的價格買花瓶，真是太蠢了。

style
[staɪl]
名 風格；文體

補充 classic 經典的
The classic style of wedding dress really fits the bride.
經典的婚紗款式真的很適合那位新娘。

subject
[`sʌbdʒɪkt]
名 主題；科目

They quickly got bored with the serious subject.
他們很快就對這個嚴肅的主題感到無聊。

subway
[`sʌb͵we]
名 地下鐵

It's foggy today, so I'd rather take the subway instead of driving.
今天霧很濃，與其開車，我寧願搭地鐵。

succeed
[sək`sid]
動 成功

My uncle succeeded in setting up a restaurant in the U.S.
我叔叔成功在美國開了一間餐廳。

success
[sək`sɛs]
名 成功

Success needs a lot of efforts and a little luck.
成功需要很多努力及一點運氣。

successful
[sək`sɛsfəl]
形 成功的

Here are some tips to host a successful party.
要辦一場成功的派對，這裡有幾個祕訣。

such
[sʌtʃ]
形 如此的；這樣的

I've never had such a delicious roast beef before.
我從來沒吃過這麼美味的烤牛肉。

sudden
[`sʌdn̩]
形 突然的

Tina was sick because of the sudden change of weather.
由於天氣驟變，蒂娜生病了。

sugar
[`ʃʊgɚ]
名 糖

Add one teaspoon of sugar could make your dish tasty.
加一茶匙糖能讓你的菜餚變美味。

suggest
[sə`dʒɛst]
動 建議；提議

I suggest that you eat something like lean meat and vegetables.
我建議你吃點像是瘦肉或蔬菜的東西。

suit
[sut]
動 適合　名 套裝

I think this polo shirt suits you well.
我覺得這件 POLO 衫很適合你。

summer
[`sʌmə]
名 夏天

Summer is the perfect time to go fishing.
夏天是最適合釣魚的季節。

sun
[sʌn]
名 太陽

To avoid sunburn, you should not stay in the sun for too long.
為了避免曬傷，不要在大太陽底下待太久。

Sunday
[`sʌnde]
名 星期日

Mother's Day is on the 2nd Sunday in May.
母親節是在五月的第二個星期天。

sunny
[`sʌnɪ]
形 晴朗的

補充 evergreen 萬年青、常綠樹
Most evergreens like a sunny position.
大多數萬年青喜歡充滿陽光的位置。

super
[`supə]
形 超級的

Billy is a super fan of that band.
比利是那個樂團的超級粉絲。

supermarket
[`supə,markɪt]
名 超級市場

Mr. Lin likes going shopping at a supermarket.
林先生喜歡去超級市場購物。

supper
[`sʌpə]
名 晚餐

Would you like to stay and have supper?
你想留下來吃晚餐嗎？

support
[səˋport]
名 動 支持

補充 technical 技術性的
Could you provide good technical support?
你能提供良好的技術支援嗎?

sure
[ʃur]
形 確定的;當然的

The clerk weighed the package to make sure how much I need to pay.
職員秤了包裹的重量,確定我該付多少錢。

surf
[sɜf]
動 衝浪;瀏覽網路 名 浪花

What a waste to stay in the shade! Let's go surfing!
待在陰涼處太可惜了!我們去衝浪吧!

surprise
[səˋpraɪz]
名 驚喜 動 使驚奇

To my surprise, she passed the examination.
令我吃驚的是,她通過了考試。

surprised
[səˋpraɪzd]
形 感到驚訝的

I'm surprised at the news about David's wedding.
大衛舉辦婚禮的消息令我感到驚訝。

survive
[səˋvaɪv]
動 倖存;存活

補充 unharmed 無恙的、沒有受傷的
They survived the accident unharmed.
他們在意外中毫髮無傷地活了下來。

swallow
[ˋswɑlo]
動 吞嚥 名 燕子

Every swimmer swallows some water at the beginning.
每一個游泳菜鳥剛開始都會喝進水的。

swan
[swɑn]
名 天鵝

補充 compose 作詞、作曲
Swan Lake was composed by Tchaikovsky.
《天鵝湖》是柴可夫斯基的作品。

sweater
[`swɛtɚ]
名 毛衣

補充 shrank 為 shrink（收縮）的過去式
My sweater shrank after my mother washed it.
母親洗過之後，我的毛衣就縮水了。

sweep
[swip]
動 名 掃

補充 三態變化為 sweep, swept, swept
My father swept the floor and I took out the garbage.
父親掃地，而我去丟垃圾。

sweet
[swit]
形 甜的

補充 sweet potato 地瓜
The plums you bought taste sweet and sour.
你買的李子嚐起來酸酸甜甜的。

swim
[swɪm]
動 游泳

補充 三態變化為 swim, swam, swum
The athlete swam 20 laps this morning.
那名運動員今天早上游了二十趟。

swimsuit
[`swɪmsut]
名 （女生的）泳衣

Lisa bought a new swimsuit for her daughter.
麗莎替女兒買了一件新泳衣。

swing
[swɪŋ]
動 名 搖動；搖擺

補充 三態變化為 swing, swung, swung
Jennifer swings her hand to say goodbye.
珍妮佛揮手道別。

symbol
[`sɪmbḷ]
名 象徵；標誌

補充 owl 貓頭鷹 / wisdom 智慧
An owl is traditionally regarded as a symbol of wisdom.
傳統上認為貓頭鷹是智慧的象徵。

system
[`sɪstəm]
名 系統

The subway system in this city is so convenient.
這座城市的地鐵系統實在太方便了。

Unit 20 Tt 字頭單字

table
[`tebl]
名 桌子；表格

Johnny folded the napkin and left it on the table after dinner.
強尼用餐完畢後將餐巾對折，置於桌上。

table tennis
片 桌球；乒乓球

Table tennis is very popular in Asian countries.
桌球在亞洲國家相當受歡迎。

tail
[tel]
名 尾巴

Candy is a black dog with white tail.
糖果是一隻有白尾巴的黑狗。

Taiwan
[taɪ`wɑn]
名 臺灣

Summer in Taiwan is usually very long and hot.
臺灣的夏季通常特別長，又很熱。

take
[tek]
動 拿；帶；採用

補充 luggage 行李
Jason checked the name tag and realized he took the wrong luggage.
傑森查看名牌，發現他拿錯行李箱了。

talent
[`tælənt]
名 天賦；才能

Mr. Lee knew my brother has a talent for painting.
李先生知道我哥哥有繪畫的天份。

talk
[tɔk]
動 講話 名 談話

補充 talk sth. out 透過協商解決問題
We've talked things out. It was just a misunderstanding.
我們把話說開了，原來都只是誤會。

talkative
[`tɔkətɪv]
形 健談的；喜歡說話的

Vivian has been talkative and active since she entered college.
進大學之後，薇薇安一直都很健談、積極。

tall
[tɔl]
形 高的

The outfit will make you look tall and slim.
這件套裝能讓你看起來高挑又纖細。

tangerine
[`tændʒə,rin]
名 橘子

補充 distinguish...from 區別
Mike couldn't distinguish tangerines from oranges.
麥克分辨不出橘子和柳橙的差別。

tank
[tæŋk]
名 坦克；槽

補充 指貯存水、油、氣等的槽或箱
What's the charge if I don't return the car with a full tank?
如果我還車時沒加滿油，費用會怎麼算呢？

tape
[tep]
名 膠帶；錄音帶

補充 scissors 剪刀
To wrap the present, Lisa took some tape and scissors.
為了包禮物，麗莎拿了膠帶和剪刀。

taste
[test]
動 品嚐

補充 cocktail 雞尾酒 / smooth 平滑的
The cocktail tastes pretty smooth.
雞尾酒嚐起來很順口。

taxi
[`tæksɪ]
名 計程車

補充 take a taxi 搭計程車
Ivy took a taxi to the airport because she was in a hurry.
艾薇很趕時間，所以她搭計程車去機場。

tea
[ti]
名 茶

In summer, a nice glass of iced tea is sure to help you beat the heat.
夏天來一杯美味的冰茶能助你消暑。

teach
[titʃ]
動 教

補充 resume 簡歷、履歷
As you can see from my resume, I have experience in teaching.
如同我履歷上寫的，我有教學經驗。

teacher
[`titʃɚ]
名 老師；教師

補充 get along well 相處得很好
My teacher is very nice and we get along well.
我的老師為人和善，我們處得很好。

team
[tim]
名 隊伍

I joined the baseball team in high school.
我高中時加入了棒球隊。

teapot
[`ti,pɑt]
名 茶壺

My aunt enjoys spending her money on beautiful teapots.
我阿姨喜歡花錢買漂亮的茶壺。

tear
[tɪr]
名 眼淚 動 撕開；扯破

補充 表「撕開」時，音標為 [tɛr]
Harvey didn't drop a tear when he broke his arm.
哈威手臂骨折時，沒有掉一滴眼淚。

teenager
[`tin,edʒɚ]
名 十幾歲的青少年

補充 have no idea 不知道
I really have no idea what teenagers are thinking.
我完全不清楚青少年的想法。

telephone
[`tɛlə,fon]
名 電話

Could you leave your name and telephone number?
可以留下您的姓名與電話號碼嗎？

television
[`tɛlə,vɪʒən]
名 電視

Tony can fix his car and television by himself.
東尼可以自己修理汽車與電視機。

tell
[tɛl]
動 告訴

To tell you the truth, I don't like big cities.
老實說，我並不喜歡大城市。

temperature
[ˋtɛmprətʃɚ]
名 溫度

The lowest temperature will be ten degrees Celsius tomorrow.
明天最低溫只有攝氏十度。

temple
[ˋtɛmpl̩]
名 廟宇；神殿

補充 worship 崇拜、敬仰
Frank goes to a temple and worship whenever he has free time.
只要有空，法蘭克就會去廟裡拜拜。

ten
[tɛn]
形 十的 名 十

Let's take a short break. I'll be back in ten minutes.
我們休息一下，十分鐘後就回來。

tennis
[ˋtɛnɪs]
名 網球

補充 network 網狀系統
A game of tennis was broadcast on a national radio network.
一場網球比賽在全國廣播網上聯播。

tent
[tɛnt]
名 帳篷

補充 pitch 搭帳篷、紮營
Kyle looked around and decided to pitch our tent here.
凱爾看了一下四周，決定在此處搭帳篷。

term
[tɝm]
名 術語；期限

I don't understand all the technical terms the man used.
我完全聽不懂那名男性使用的專業術語。

terrible
[ˋtɛrəbl̩]
形 可怕的；糟糕的

I feel terrible that I forgot my father's birthday.
忘了父親生日讓我感覺糟透了。

terrific
[təˋrɪfɪk]
形 非常好的；驚人的

Did you go to his concert last night? It was terrific.
我昨晚有去他的演唱會嗎？真是棒呆了。

test
[tɛst]
名 考試 動 測驗

補充 a piece of cake 容易的事
The test was a piece of cake for Annie.
那個考試對安妮來說太容易了。

textbook
[ˋtɛkstˌbʊk]
名 教科書

補充 refer to 參考、提到
If you have questions, you can refer to the textbooks.
有問題的話，你可以參考課本。

than
介 超過 連 比較

There are more than 30 student clubs in our school.
我們學校的社團數量超過三十個。

thank
[θæŋk]
動 感謝

Thanks for inviting me. See you then.
謝謝你邀請我，我們到時候見。

Thanksgiving
[ˌθæŋksˋgɪvɪŋ]
名 感恩節

補充 gathering 聚會、集會
Thanksgiving is a day for family gatherings for Americans.
對美國人來說，感恩節是家人聚會的日子。

that
[ðæt]
形 那個 連 以致
代 那個（人或事）

I know a friend who works for that company.
我認識的一個朋友在那間公司上班。

the
[ðə]
冠 這個；那個

補充 get to the point 講重點
Ms. Chen asked her colleagues to get to the point.
陳小姐要求她的同事直接說重點。

theater
[`θɪətɚ]
名 電影院;劇院

補充 performance 表演、演出
The Cloud Gate will give a performance at an open-air theater.
雲門舞集將在露天劇場進行演出。

their
[ðɛr]
限 他們的(所有格)

補充 theirs 他們的(東西)
Passengers should check in at least two hours before their flight time.
乘客必須在起飛前兩個小時完成登機手續。

then
[ðɛn]
副 之後;當時

補充 blow out 吹熄
You can make a wish, and then blow out the candles.
你可以先許願,再吹熄蠟燭。

there
[ðɛr]
副 在那裡

The girl over there is my elder sister.
在那裡的女生是我姐姐。

therefore
[`ðɛr,for]
副 因此

補充 show off 賣弄、炫耀
Joe likes to show off; therefore, he has no friends.
喬喜歡炫耀,所以沒有朋友。

these
[ðiz]
形 這些的 代 這些

There is an underpass connecting these two streets.
有一個地下道連接這兩條街。

they
[ðe]
代 他們;她們;它們

補充 them 他們(受格)/ themselves 他們自己
My parents are Catholic and they go to Mass every Sunday.
我父母信天主教,每個星期天都去望彌撒。

thick
[θɪk]
形 粗的;厚的

It's too cold to go outside without a thick jacket.
外面太冷了,沒有穿厚外套無法出門。

thief
[θif]
名 小偷

The thief was caught by the police.
那名小偷被警方抓住了。

thin
[θɪn]
形 薄的；瘦的

This piece of paper is too thin.
這張紙太薄了。

thing
[θɪŋ]
名 事物；東西

Going to the beach is the most fun thing about summer.
夏天去海邊是最有趣的事了。

think
[θɪŋk]
動 想；思考；認為

I think the purse is the best deal of the annual sale.
我覺得這個皮包是週年慶商品中最划算的。

third
[θɝd]
形 第三的

The machine has broken down again. This is the third time this month.
這台機器又壞了，這是這個月第三次了。

thirsty
[`θɝstɪ]
形 口渴的

I am thirsty. Can you give me some water, please?
我很渴，能不能請你給我一些水喝？

thirteen
[θɝ`tin]
形 十三的 名 十三

補充 profit 利潤
The company's profits declined about thirteen percent.
公司利潤下滑了百分之十三左右。

thirty
[`θɝtɪ]
形 三十的 名 三十

There were thirty minutes left before the airplane departed.
在飛機起飛之前，有三十分鐘的時間。

this
[ðɪs]
形 代 這；這個

You have to take this medicine after each meal.
你每餐飯後都必須服用這個藥。

those
[ðoz]
形 那些的 代 那些

Those employees are blue-collar workers.
那些員工是藍領階級的工人。

though
[ðo]
連 雖然 副 然而

Though I look older, I'm actually the youngest of the three.
雖然我看起來比較老，但我其實是三人當中最年輕的。

thousand
[`θauznd]
形 一千的 名 一千

補充 attract 吸引、引起（注意等）
This event attracts thousands of people every year.
這場盛會每年都會吸引好幾千人來。

three
[θri]
形 三的 名 三

I try to go to the gym two to three times a week.
我盡量每個星期健身兩到三次。

throat
[θrot]
名 喉嚨

補充 wake up 醒來
I woke up yesterday with a sore throat and a fever.
昨天早上起床，發現自己喉嚨痛又發燒。

through
[θru]
介 副 通過；穿過

John has always wanted to go backpacking through Europe.
約翰一直都很想自助旅行，遊遍歐洲。

throw
[θro]
動 投；拋

補充 三態為 throw, threw, thrown
Victor quickly threw the ball to the forward.
維克多迅速把球傳給前鋒。

thumb
[θʌm]
名 拇指

The girl bit the tip of her right thumb, looking at me.
這個女孩咬著右手拇指的指尖看著我。

thunder
[`θʌndə]
名 雷

補充 a clap of thunder 打雷隆隆的聲響
There was a clap of thunder striking from the cloudy sky.
一聲雷鳴劃破烏雲密布的天空。

Thursday
[`θɜzde]
名 星期四

Thanksgiving Day is celebrated on the fourth Thursday in November.
十一月的第四個星期四會慶祝感恩節。

ticket
[`tɪkɪt]
名 票；罰單

補充 reserve 保留 / concert 音樂會
I've reserved two tickets for tonight's piano concert.
我已經預訂了兩張今晚鋼琴演奏會的門票。

tidy
[`taɪdɪ]
動 整理 形 整潔的

補充 tidy up 收拾、整理
As soon as he got his wife's call, he went to tidy the room up.
他接到太太的電話之後，就開始收拾房間。

tie
[taɪ]
動 打結 名 領帶

補充 三態變化為 tie, tied, tied
Susan tied a ribbon around the box.
蘇珊在盒子上繫了一個緞帶。

tiger
[`taɪgə]
名 老虎

This brave hunter killed a tiger last summer.
這名英勇的獵人去年夏天殺死了一隻老虎。

till
[tɪl]
介 連 直到…為止

補充 同義詞有 until / reservation 預訂
Your reservation will be kept till two o'clock tomorrow.
您的訂位會保留到明天兩點。

time
[taɪm]
名 時間；次數

Christmas holidays are the time for decorating and celebrating.
聖誕假期就是要來裝飾和慶祝的時間。

tiny
[`taɪnɪ]
形 微小的；極小的

補充 vitality 活力、生命力
The tiny plant shows strong vitality.
這株小植物展現出強大的生命力。

tip
[tɪp]
名 小費；尖端 動 給小費

Ben was hoping the customer would leave a big tip.
班原本寄望客人會給很多小費。

tired
[taɪrd]
形 疲倦的

Sean was tired after staying up all night.
尚恩整個晚上都沒睡，因此感到很疲倦。

title
[`taɪtl̩]
名 標題；頭銜

補充 bold 粗筆畫的
Please add a bold line under the title.
請在標題下方加一條粗線。

to
[tu]
介 到；向；朝

補充 to 常與動詞合用，形成不定詞用法
Just grab my hand. I'll lead you to the other side of the pool.
抓住我的手，我會帶你去泳池的另一邊。

toast
[tost]
名 吐司麵包 動 烤麵包

Please butter a piece of toast for the guest.
請幫客人的一片吐司麵包塗上奶油。

today
[tə`de]
副 名 今天

I don't want to go out today because the wind is blowing hard outside.
今天外面風好大，所以我不想出門。

toe
[to]
名 腳趾

Frank kicked the vending machine hard and hurt his toes.
法蘭克用力踢了這台自動販賣機，傷到他的腳趾。

tofu
[`tofu]
名 豆腐

Stinky tofu is too much for most foreigners.
臭豆腐對大多數外國人來說太刺激了。

together
[tə`gɛðə]
副 一起地

Family members would get together and eat a big meal on that day.
我家人們會在那天聚在一起吃大餐。

toilet
[`tɔɪlɪt]
名 廁所；馬桶

I need to go to the toilet before the film starts.
在電影開始之前，我想要先去上廁所。

tomato
[tə`meto]
名 番茄

My mother put bananas and tomatoes on the counter.
我媽媽把香蕉和番茄放到櫃檯上。

tomorrow
[tə`mɔro]
副 名 明天

It will be mostly cloudy with a high temperature tomorrow.
明天天氣很可能是高溫的陰天。

tongue
[tʌŋ]
名 舌頭

補充 nostril 鼻孔
The doctor checked the girl's tongue and nostrils.
醫生檢查了女孩的舌頭和鼻孔。

tonight
[tə`naɪt]
副 名 今晚

補充 conductor 指揮
The conductor is going to direct a band of 100 people tonight.
這名指揮家今晚將指揮一個百人樂團。

too
[tu]
副 也;過於

補充 split up 分離
Some couples split up because their personalities are too different.
有些情侶會因為個性相差太多而分開。

tool
[tul]
名 工具

補充 aisle 通道、走道
All the drawing tools are in the second aisle.
繪畫的工具都放在第二條走道。

tooth
[tuθ]
名 牙齒

補充 cavity 蛀洞
Ann went to see the dentist because it was a cavity in her tooth.
安的牙齒有個蛀洞,所以去看牙醫。

toothache
[`tuθ,ek]
名 牙痛

補充 chew 咀嚼
I have problem chewing because of a toothache.
因為牙痛,所以我咀嚼有困難。

toothbrush
[`tuθ,brʌʃ]
名 牙刷

Please remember to pack me a toothbrush.
請記得幫我打包一支牙刷。

top
[tap]
形 頂端的 名 頂部;上方

He lives on the 21st floor, the top floor of this building.
他住在二十一樓,這棟建築物的頂樓。

topic
[`tapɪk]
名 主題;題目

The topic of her research is very similar to mine.
她研究的主題和我的非常類似。

total
[`totḷ]
形 全部的 名 總數

The quiz takes only ten percent of the total grade.
這個測驗只占總成績的百分之十。

touch
[tʌtʃ]
動 觸碰 **名** 接觸

補充 keep in touch with sb. 與某人保持聯繫
She **touched** her son's face to make sure he was crying.
她觸摸兒子的臉龐，確定他在哭。

toward
[tə`wɔrd]
介 向；對

We should always remain a positive attitude **toward** the future.
無論何時，我們都應該對未來抱持著積極的態度。

towel
[`tauəl]
名 毛巾

I need one more **towel** and some soap.
我還需要一條毛巾和肥皂。

tower
[`tauə]
名 塔

補充 spiral 螺旋形的 / staircase 樓梯
We climbed the spiral staircase to the **tower**.
我們爬上通往塔樓的螺旋梯。

town
[taun]
名 城鎮

When the winter comes, the swallows leave the **town**.
冬天來時，燕子會飛離小鎮。

toy
[tɔɪ]
名 玩具

補充 put sth. away 放好、歸位
You'd better put the **toys** away before the guests come.
在客人們抵達之前，你最好把玩具收拾好。

trace
[tres]
動 追蹤 **名** 蹤跡

Kim **traced** the footprints and then found out who the thief was.
金追蹤著足跡，發現了小偷的真面目。

trade
[tred]
動 交易 **名** 貿易

Mr. Wang has been **trading** in furniture for ten years.
王先生從事傢俱買賣十年了。

tradition
[trə`dɪʃən]
名 傳統

According to the tradition, people should not sleep on New Year's Eve.
根據傳統，除夕夜不可以睡覺。

traditional
[trə`dɪʃənḷ]
形 傳統的

The festival is to celebrate the Taiwanese traditional culture.
這次活動是為了頌揚臺灣傳統文化。

traffic
[`træfɪk]
名 交通

補充 congestion 擁塞、擠滿
Jason doesn't like the traffic congestion of city life.
傑森不喜歡交通擁擠的都市生活。

train
[tren]
名 火車 動 訓練

補充 timetable（火車等的）時刻表
We looked at the timetable and realized that the train had departed.
我們看了時刻表，意識到火車已經開走了。

trap
[træp]
動 誘捕 名 陷阱；圈套

The hunter used a piece of meat to trap the wolf.
獵人以肉塊來誘捕野狼。

trash
[`træʃ]
名 垃圾

補充 a bag of trash 一袋垃圾
My sister and I took out the trash after dinner.
我姐姐和我晚餐後去倒了垃圾。

travel
[`trævḷ]
動 旅行 名 旅遊

補充 astronaut 太空人
My dream is to become an astronaut and travel to Mars.
我的夢想是成為太空人，到火星旅行。

treasure
[`trɛʒɚ]
名 財寶 動 珍愛

補充 literary 文學的
I spent hours in a bookstore looking for literary treasures.
我花了好幾個小時在書店找文學珍寶。

treat
[trit]
動 對待；治療 **名** 款待

My parents treat us as friends.
我父母待我們像朋友一樣。

tree
[tri]
名 樹木

Let's decorate the Christmas tree together!
讓我們一起來裝飾聖誕樹吧！

triangle
[`traɪˌæŋgl̩]
名 三角形

補充 trunk 汽車行李箱
We have an emergency road triangle in our trunk.
我們的後車箱有放一個三角警示牌。

trick
[trɪk]
名 詭計；戲法 **動** 哄騙

The magician promised to teach him a few tricks.
那名魔術師承諾要教他幾個戲法。

trip
[trɪp]
名 旅行

補充 unforgettable 難忘的
My last trip with friends left me with unforgettable memories.
我最後一次和朋友旅行的回憶令人難忘。

trouble
[`trʌbl̩]
名 麻煩

補充 get involved in 涉足、牽扯
I don't want to get involved in this trouble.
我不想被牽扯進這個麻煩中。

trousers
[`traʊzɚz]
名 長褲

補充 a pair of 一對、一雙、一條
I bought a new pair of trousers for my brother.
我替我哥哥買了一件新長褲。

truck
[trʌk]
名 卡車

補充 dump 傾倒 / load 裝載量 / log 原木
The truck dumped its load of logs on the ground.
卡車將裝載的原木卸在地上。

true
[tru]
形 真實的;正確的

補充 liar 騙子、說謊的人
Don't call me a liar. What I said was true.
別叫我騙子,我說的是真的。

trumpet
[`trʌmpɪt]
名 小喇叭 動 吹喇叭

Daniel plays the trumpet in the military band.
丹尼爾在軍樂隊中吹奏小喇叭。

trust
[trʌst]
動 名 信任

Samantha trusted her father on every decision he made.
她父親做的每一個決定,莎曼珊都信得過。

truth
[truθ]
名 事實;真相

補充 be tired of 對…感到厭倦
Lucas is tired of hiding the truth.
路卡斯對隱藏真相感到厭煩。

try
[traɪ]
動 名 嘗試

補充 cheer up 高興起來 / deal with 處理
Oliver tried to cheer up and deal with the problems.
奧利佛試著打起精神,處理那些問題。

T-shirt
[`ti.ʃɜt]
名 T恤

補充 washable 可洗的
The T-shirts and pants are machine washable.
那幾件 T 恤和長褲都能用機器水洗。

tub
[tʌb]
名 盆;桶

補充 brighten 使明亮
Tubs planted with flowers brightened the yard.
栽種花盆使庭院明亮了起來。

tube
[tjub]
名 管子

補充 inner 內部的
I can replace my bike tires and inner tubes on my own.
我會自己更換腳踏車的車輪和內胎。

Tuesday
[`tjuzde]
名 星期二

We should know by next Tuesday whom we will hire.
下週二之前我們應該就知道會錄取誰了。

tunnel
[`tʌnḷ]
名 隧道

We passed through several tunnels before we reached the village.
穿過了幾條隧道，我們才抵達那個村莊。

turkey
[`t3kɪ]
名 火雞

Turkey and pumpkin pie are common foods on Thanksgiving Day.
火雞和南瓜派是感恩節上常見的食物。

turn
[t3n]
動 名 轉動；旋轉

Remember to face your audience; don't turn your back on them.
記得要面對你的觀眾，不要背對他們。

turtle
[`t3tḷ]
名 烏龜

補充 float 漂浮、浮動
There were two turtles floating on the sea.
有兩隻海龜漂浮在海上。

twelve
[twɛlv]
形 十二的 名 十二

補充 battery 電池
The battery of my laptop lasts up to twelve hours.
我筆電的電池可以支撐十二個小時。

twenty
[`twɛntɪ]
形 二十的 名 二十

補充 keep in touch 保持聯絡
Ms. Lee and her stepmother kept in touch by e-mail for twenty years.
李小姐與繼母以電子郵件保持聯繫二十年。

twice
[twaɪs]
副 兩次

My family and I usually travel abroad once or twice a year.
家人和我通常一年出國旅行一到兩次。

two
[tu]
形 二的　名 二

Each person is allowed to carry two pieces of luggage.
每個人可以攜帶兩件行李。

type
[taɪp]
名 類型　動 打字

What type of service do you offer?
你們提供什麼類型的服務呢？

typhoon
[taɪ`fun]
名 颱風

補充 mudflow 土石流 / landslide 山崩
Typhoons also cause mudflows and landslides.
颱風也會造成土石流與山崩。

Unit 21　Uu 字頭單字

MP3 21

ugly
[`ʌglɪ]
形 醜的

I think the color of this dress is really ugly.
我覺得這件洋裝的顏色很醜。

umbrella
[ʌm`brɛlə]
名 雨傘

補充 folding 可摺疊的
I have a folding umbrella in my backpack.
我在背包裡放了一支折傘。

uncle
[`ʌŋkḷ]
名 叔叔；舅舅；伯伯

Sandy visited her uncle and gave him the invitation in person.
珊蒂拜訪了她舅舅，將邀請函親手交給他。

under
[`ʌndə]
介 在…下面；低於

補充 snorkel 浮潛
It's great to take photos when snorkeling under water.
浮潛時拍照是很棒的一件事。

underline
[,ʌndə`laɪn]
動 劃底線 名 底線

To remind herself, Lily underlined the date for the party.
為了提醒自己，莉莉在派對日期下劃線。

underpass
[`ʌndə,pæs]
名 地下道

The underpass has been closed for three days through flooding.
由於淹水，這條地下道已被封閉了三天。

understand
[,ʌndə`stænd]
動 了解

補充 essay 論說文
After reading the essay, I understood his key points.
閱讀這篇文章後，我理解他的重點了。

underwear
[`ʌndə,wɛr]
名 內衣

補充 take off 脫去衣物、飛機起飛
The nurse asked me to take off my underwear and lie down.
護士要求我脫下內衣並躺下。

unhappy
[ʌn`hæpɪ]
形 不快樂的

The workers are unhappy about the working environment.
員工們不怎麼喜歡工作環境。

uniform
[`junə,fɔrm]
名 制服

補充 flight attendant 空服員
The flight attendants all look very much alike in uniform.
穿著制服的空服員們看起來都好像。

unique
[ju`nik]
形 獨特的

The way she handles her work and leads her team is unique.
她處理事情及領導團隊的方式是獨一無二的。

universe
[`junə,vɜs]
名 宇宙

補充 astronomer 天文學家
Early astronomers thought that the earth was the center of the universe.
早期的天文學家認為地球是宇宙的中心。

university
[,junə`vɜsətɪ]
名 大學

He got his Ph.D. degree last year and is teaching in a university now.
他去年拿到博士學位的文憑，現在在大學教書。

until
[ən`tɪl]
連 介 直到…時

補充 conference 會議
Our manager won't be available until the conference is finished.
我們經理要到會議結束之後才有空。

up
[ʌp]
副 向上地 介 在…之上

My daughter is only one year old, but she can count up to ten.
我女兒才一歲，但她能從一數到十。

upload
[ʌp`lod]
動 上傳（檔案）名 上傳

Please upload your file to the network hard drive.
請將你的檔案上傳到網路硬碟。

upon
[ə`pɑn]
介 在…上面

補充 once upon a time 很久以前
Once upon a time, there was a giant who had a golden bird.
從前有個巨人，他有一隻金鳥。

upper
[`ʌpɚ]
形 在上面的；較高的

I have something like a rash all over my back and upper arms.
我的背部和上臂都長了類似紅疹的東西。

upstairs
[`ʌp`stɛrz]
副 在樓上
名 樓上 形 樓上的

If you're looking for Henry, he is studying upstairs.
如果你要找亨利，他正在樓上唸書。

USA / U.S.A.
縮 美國

補充 完整拼法為 United States of America
The TV station has several correspondents in the U.S.A.
這家電視臺在美國有幾位特派員。

use
[juz]
動 利用 名 用途

The air conditioner isn't working. Please use the fans.
冷氣壞了，請使用電風扇。

useful
[`jusfəl]
形 有用的

Adam found several useful camping tips on a website.
亞當在網站上找到幾個實用的露營撇步。

usual
[`juʒuəl]
形 平常的

John always wears his usual white T-shirt and blue jeans.
約翰總是穿著他平常的白 T 恤與藍牛仔褲。

Unit 22 Vv 字頭單字

MP3 22

vacation
[ve`keʃən]
名 假期

I went nowhere in my summer vacation this year.
我今年暑假哪裡都沒去。

Valentine
[`væləntaɪn]
名 情人節

Lovers would celebrate their love on Valentine's Day.
情侶會在情人節這一天慶祝兩人的愛情。

valley
[ˋvælɪ]
名 山谷

They were trapped in the valley by the heavy snow.
他們被大風雪困在山谷中。

valuable
[ˋvæljʊəb!]
形 貴重的

Are there any valuable things in your bag?
你的袋子裡有什麼貴重物品嗎？

value
[ˋvælju]
名 價值 動 評價

The owner of the old furniture didn't realize its value until we told him.
在我們告訴他之前，這件舊傢俱的主人並不知道它的價值有多少。

vegetable
[ˋvɛdʒətəb!]
名 蔬菜

補充 variety 多樣化、各種各樣
The produce department offers a great variety of fruits and vegetables.
農產區有各式各樣的水果和蔬菜可挑。

vendor
[ˋvɛndɚ]
名 攤販

The vendor at the corner was a school teacher.
那名在街角的攤販原本是一位老師。

very
[ˋvɛrɪ]
副 很；非常

Kevin always makes me laugh. He is very humorous.
凱文總能讓我大笑，他實在很幽默。

vest
[vɛst]
名 背心

Although the vest fit her nicely, she didn't like it.
雖然那件背心很合身，但她並不喜歡。

victory
[ˋvɪktərɪ]
名 勝利

補充 tough 嚴格的、強硬的
The victory came after three years of tough training.
苦練了三年，終於贏得勝利。

video
[`vɪdɪˏo]
名 錄影

補充 refundable 可退還的
Things like movies, music and video games are not refundable.
電影、音樂和電動遊戲是不能退款的。

village
[`vɪlɪdʒ]
名 村落

I was born into a family of five in a small village in Chiayi.
我出生於嘉義的小村莊，一個五人的家庭。

vinegar
[`vɪnɪgɚ]
名 醋

補充 flavor 給⋯調味
My mother flavored the fish with sugar and vinegar.
我媽媽用糖和醋給魚調味。

violin
[ˏvaɪəˋlɪn]
名 小提琴

I learned the violin for a while, but I was not good at it.
我學過一陣子小提琴，但拉得不好。

visit
[`vɪzɪt]
動 名 參觀；訪問

Don't forget to send me a postcard when you visit Canada.
當你到加拿大時，別忘了給我寄封明信片。

visitor
[`vɪzɪtɚ]
名 訪客；遊客

補充 exhibition 展覽
We had some visitors from Hong Kong attending our exhibition.
有幾位來自香港的訪客參與我們的展覽。

vocabulary
[vəˋkæbjəˏlɛrɪ]
名 字彙

Ted memorizes the vocabularies for the test tomorrow.
為了明天的考試，泰德背誦單字。

voice
[vɔɪs]
名 （人的）聲音

補充 mute 消除（聲音）/ show up 出現
The students began to mute their voices when the teacher showed up.
老師一出現，學生們立刻安靜下來。

volleyball
[`vɑlɪ,bɔl]
名 排球

Playing beach volleyball is a great way to meet new friends.
打沙灘排球是認識新朋友的好方法。

vote
[vot]
動 投票

補充 senator 參議員
Fifteen senators voted for the policy.
有十五位參議員投票支持這個政策。

Unit 23 Ww 字頭單字

MP3 23

waist
[west]
名 腰部

補充 elastic 有彈力的 / strap 帶子
Lisa bought a skirt with elastic straps at the waist.
麗莎買了一件腰間有鬆緊帶的裙子。

wait
[wet]
動 等候

補充 recipe 食譜
I can't wait to try your recipes.
我迫不及待地想試試你的食譜。

waiter
[`wetɚ]
名 男服務生

The waiter cleared the table after the guests finished their meals.
那群客人吃飽後,服務生便清理餐桌。

waitress
[`wetrɪs]
名 女服務生

補充 tuition fees 學費
Laura works part-time as a waitress to pay her tuition fees.
為了繳學費,蘿拉打工做女服務生。

wake
[wek]
動 叫醒

補充 wake sb. up 叫醒某人
Please wake me up at 7 o'clock tomorrow morning.
明天早上七點鐘請叫醒我。

walk
[wɔk]
動 走路

補充 detector 探測器 / beep 作嗶嗶聲
The metal detector beeps as the man walks through.
男子通過時,金屬探測器響了。

Walkman
[`wɔkmən]
名 隨身聽

Nowadays, it's rare to find someone using a Walkman.
現在很少看到有人使用隨身聽了。

wall
[wɔl]
名 牆壁

補充 crack 裂縫 / immediately 立即
The walls have got cracks and need painting immediately.
牆壁上有裂縫,需要馬上重新粉刷。

wallet
[`wɑlɪt]
名 皮夾

補充 come to one's senses 找回理智
Lisa came to her senses and decided not to buy the wallet.
麗莎恢復理智,決定不買那個皮夾了。

want
[wɑnt]
動 想要

Do you want to have a cup of coffee?
你想要喝一杯咖啡嗎?

war
[wɔr]
名 戰爭

It is reported that over 200 soldiers were killed in the war.
據報導,這場戰爭中超過兩百名士兵喪命。

warm
[wɔrm]
形 溫暖的 **動** 使暖和

補充 warm up 暖身 / dive 潛水
Diving in the warm Caribbean Sea must be a great pleasure.
在溫暖的加勒比海潛水肯定很享受。

wash
[waʃ]
動 洗

Make sure you use cold water while washing the pan.
清洗這個平底鍋時，要確保用的是冷水。

waste
[west]
動 名 浪費

Don't waste time telling your audience what they already know.
不要浪費時間講觀眾原本就知道的事。

watch
[watʃ]
動 注視；留意 名 手錶

Someone rang the doorbell while we were watching TV.
當我們在看電視時，有人按了門鈴。

water
[`wɔtɚ]
名 水

補充 frequently 頻繁地
Please drink water frequently after taking the medicine.
服用這種藥物後，請多喝水。

waterfall
[`wɔtɚ͵fɔl]
名 瀑布

I've never seen a waterfall like this. Let's take a photo!
我從沒看過這種瀑布，我們來拍張照吧！

watermelon
[`wɔtɚ͵mɛlən]
名 西瓜

Watermelon is one of my favorite fruits in summer.
西瓜是我最愛的夏季水果之一。

wave
[wev]
動 揮動 名 波浪

We waved goodbye and then got on the different buses.
我們揮手道別，分別搭上不同的公車。

way
[we]
名 方法；道路

補充 coupon 優惠券
Using coupons is a great way to save money.
使用折價券是省錢的好方法。

we
[wi]
代 我們

補充 us 我們（受格）/ ourselves 我們自己
We provide repairs during the warranty period.
保固期間我們會提供維修服務。

weak
[wik]
形 虛弱的；脆弱的

She moved the heater closer to the weak man.
她把暖氣機移得更靠近那位虛弱的男人。

wear
[wεr]
動 穿戴；磨損

補充 三態變化為 wear, wore, worn
The man wearing glasses is my husband.
戴眼鏡的男性是我的老公。

weather
[`wεðɚ]
名 天氣

補充 weather forecast 天氣預報
Did you see the weather forecast today?
你看了今天的天氣預報嗎？

Wednesday
[`wεnzde]
名 星期三

補充 tutor 家庭教師
My math tutor arranged a three-hour review this Wednesday.
我的數學家教本週三安排了三小時的複習。

week
[wik]
名 星期

How much is it if I rent a mid-size car for a week?
租中型車一個星期的費用是多少呢？

weekday
[`wik.de]
名 平日；工作日

補充 weekday 指的是扣除週末的日子
That cafeteria is open only on weekdays.
那家自助餐館只在平日開店。

weekend
[`wi.kεnd]
名 週末

We should have a meeting about the project this weekend.
我們這個週末應該針對這個計畫開會。

weight
[wet]
名 重量

補充 lose/gain weight 減少 / 增加體重
If you continue to exercise, you will lose weight and be fit.
如果你持續運動，就能減肥、維持身材。

welcome
[`wɛlkəm]
形 受歡迎的 動 歡迎

You are always welcome to come at any time.
無論任何時候，都歡迎你過來。

well
[wɛl]
副 良好地 形 健康的

補充 cooperate 合作、協作
My co-workers and I cooperate very well together.
我同事和我合作無間。

west
[wɛst]
副 向西方
形 西方的 名 西方

We are going west to the beach.
我們正朝西前往海灘。

wet
[wɛt]
形 潮溼的

I got wet. Let me change my wet clothes first.
我全身都溼了，讓我先換掉溼透的衣服。

whale
[hwel]
名 鯨魚

Have you ever been whale watching?
你有賞過鯨嗎？

what
[hwɑt]
代 什麼

I don't need a shopping list because I always know what I need.
我不需要購物清單，因為我總是很清楚自己要買什麼。

wheel
[hwil]
名 輪子

補充 coach 客運、遊覽車
The coach needs changing all four wheels.
這輛遊覽車四個輪子都需要更換。

when
[hwɛn]
連 當…時 代 何時

You can see the ocean from the balcony when the weather is clear.
天氣好的話，你能從陽臺看到海洋的景色。

where
[hwɛr]
副 在哪裡 代 …的地方

Excuse me; where is the nearest post office?
不好意思，最近的郵局在哪裡呢？

whether
[`hwɛðɚ]
連 是否

I'm not sure whether the style is fashionable this year.
我不確定這個風格今年是否會流行。

which
[hwɪtʃ]
代 哪一個

I am not quite sure which pair of shoes to wear.
我不太確定要穿哪一雙鞋子。

while
[hwaɪl]
連 當…的時候 名 一會兒

補充 contest 比賽、競爭
I won the first prize in a speech contest while in college.
在大學時，我獲得演講比賽第一名。

white
[hwaɪt]
形 白色的 名 白色

I'd like some white wine to go with the chicken.
我想點白酒來配雞肉。

who
[hu]
代 誰；什麼人

We bought some souvenirs as gifts for those who did not make the trip.
我們買了一些紀念品，送給沒能參加旅遊的人當禮物。

whole
[hol]
形 完整的；全部的

It usually takes more than five hours to roast a whole turkey.
烤一整隻火雞通常需要五個多小時的時間。

whose
[huz]
代 誰的

Ms. Yang has a three-month-old baby whose name is Ben.
楊小姐有個三個月大的嬰兒，他叫做班。

why
[hwaɪ]
副 為什麼

補充 thoroughly 徹底地
Why didn't you thoroughly check the data?
你為什麼沒有徹底檢查資料的內容呢？

wide
[waɪd]
形 寬的；廣泛的

補充 a wide range of …範圍很廣
The rental shop offers a wide range of bikes to rent.
那輛租車店有各種類型的腳踏車可租。

wife
[waɪf]
名 妻子

Daniel's wife is two years younger than him.
丹尼爾的太太比他小兩歲。

wild
[waɪld]
形 野生的

補充 poisonous 有毒的
Many wild berries are poisonous and would make you sick.
很多野莓有毒，會讓你生病。

will
[wɪl]
助 將；會

補充 delay 使延期、耽擱
Your flight will be delayed for 50 minutes.
你的班機會延誤五十分鐘。

win
[wɪn]
動 贏得；獲勝

補充 三態變化為 win, won, won
If I won the lottery, I would travel around the world.
如果我中了樂透，我就要環遊世界。

wind
[wɪnd]
名 風 動 上緊發條

補充 wind 當動詞時，音標為 [waɪnd]
The wind scattered the files to the floor.
風把文件吹散到地上。

window
[`wɪndo]
名 窗戶

補充 perch 使飛落、暫歇
A blackbird perched on the branches outside my window.
一隻燕八哥棲息在我窗戶外面的樹枝上。

windy
[`wɪndɪ]
形 多風的

This cold and windy weather is very common in January.
這麼冷又起風的天氣在一月是很常見的。

wing
[wɪŋ]
名 翅膀

The eagle has wings that spread 2 meters.
這隻老鷹展翼的翅膀有兩公尺。

winner
[`wɪnɚ]
名 贏家；勝利者

補充 panel 評判小組 / finale 結尾
A panel of judges will select the winner in the season finale.
評審團將於本季最後一集選出冠軍。

winter
[`wɪntɚ]
名 冬天；冬季

Judy has gained five pounds since last winter.
從去年冬天開始，茱蒂胖了五磅。

wise
[waɪz]
形 有智慧的

Bill is a wise man; he's never affected by people's opinions.
比爾是名智者，他從不被他人意見左右。

wish
[wɪʃ]
動 許願 名 願望

I wish I had the money to buy all the books I like.
真希望我有錢，能買下所有我喜歡的書。

with
[wɪð]
介 帶有；具有

補充 diagnose 診斷
If you have been diagnosed with the flu, you should stay home.
如果你被診斷出感染病毒，就應該待在家。

without
[wɪ`ðaʊt]
介 沒有

Haven't you heard that she can drink a lot without getting drunk?
你沒聽說她喝很多酒都不會醉嗎？

wok
[wɑk]
名 中式炒菜鍋

You will need a wok if you want to make Chinese food.
如果你想做中式料理，就必須準備炒菜鍋。

wolf
[wʊlf]
名 狼

補充 howl 嗥叫
I didn't sleep well because the wolves howled the whole night.
那些狼整夜嗥叫，害我沒睡好。

woman
[`wʊmən]
名 女性

The woman wearing a ponytail is my elder sister.
那個綁著馬尾的女性是我姐姐。

women's room
片 女廁

補充 也可以寫成 ladies' room
Do you know where the women's room is?
你知道女廁在哪裡嗎？

wonderful
[`wʌndəfəl]
形 很棒的；奇妙的

This necklace would be a wonderful birthday gift for my wife.
這串項鍊對我太太來說，會是很棒的生日禮物。

wood
[wʊd]
名 木材

補充 bracelet 手環 / bead 有孔小珠
We sent our grandmother a bracelet made of wood beads.
我們送奶奶一串用木珠做成的手環。

woods
[wʊdz]
名 樹林

補充 woods 通常指較小型的樹林
We went for a walk in the oak woods after lunch.
中餐過後，我們去橡樹林散步。

259

word
[wɝd]
名 單字

The little boy was too nervous to say a word.
那名小男孩太緊張了，什麼話都說不出。

work
[wɝk]
動 工作；運轉
名 工作；作品

Ben is working on a big project which gives him a lot of pressure.
班正在做一份重要的計畫，讓他倍感壓力。

workbook
[`wɝk͵bʊk]
名 （學生）練習簿

Besides the textbook, I also bought the workbook.
除了教科書以外，我還買了練習簿。

worker
[`wɝkɚ]
名 工人

補充 condition 情況
The worker is upset about the working conditions in the factory.
那名工人對工廠內的環境感到不滿。

world
[wɝld]
名 世界

補充 disaster 災難
It is a disaster movie about the end of the world.
這是一部關於世界末日的災難電影。

worm
[wɝm]
名 蠕蟲

My sister is not afraid of worms.
我妹妹不怕蟲。

worry
[`wɝɪ]
動 擔心

補充 reoccur （尤指壞事）再次發生
He is worried that the cancer might reoccur.
他很擔心癌症會再復發。

wound
[wund]
名 傷口 動 傷害

補充 scratch 抓、搔 / infect 感染
Don't scratch it, or you will infect the wound.
不要抓，不然傷口可能會感染。

wrist
[rɪst]
名 手腕

Lisa likes to wear colorful bracelets on her wrists.
麗莎喜歡在手腕上戴色彩鮮豔的手環。

write
[raɪt]
動 寫

I don't know how to write my address in English.
我不知道該怎麼用英文寫我的地址。

writer
[`raɪtɚ]
名 作家

補充 imaginative 有想像力的
She is an imaginative writer and wrote a lot of children's books.
她是個很有想像力的作家，寫了很多童書。

wrong
[rɔŋ]
形 錯誤的

It seems that you have taken the wrong train.
你似乎搭錯火車了。

Unit 24 Yy 字頭單字

MP3 24

yard
[jɑrd]
名 庭院；碼（3英尺）

The family moved in a house with a yard.
那家人搬進一間有院子的房屋。

year
[jɪr]
名 年

My brother is only one year older than me.
我哥哥只比我大一歲。

yell
[jɛl]
動 吼叫；大叫

補充 yell at 對…大叫 / umpire 裁判
The fans were yelling at the umpire.
粉絲們對著裁判吼叫。

yellow
[`jɛlo]
形 黃色的 名 黃色

Who is the boy with the blue cap and yellow jacket?
那個戴藍帽子、穿黃色夾克的男孩是誰？

yes
[jɛs]
副 是的 名 是

Yes, I do know her. She was one of my colleagues.
是的，我的確認識她，她是我以前的同事。

yesterday
[`jɛstɚde]
副 名 昨天

Our company announced yesterday that Mr. Chen has been promoted.
公司昨天宣布陳先生獲得升職。

yet
[jɛt]
副 尚未；但是 連 然而

It hasn't been decided yet when the plane will take off.
尚未決定飛機何時起飛。

you
[ju]
代 你；你們

補充 yourself 你自己 / yourselves 你們自己
Could you tell me the bus number to downtown?
你能告訴我去市中心的是幾號公車嗎？

young
[jʌŋ]
形 年輕的

The young swimmer won the competition.
那位年輕的泳者贏得了比賽。

your
[juɚ]
限 你的；你們的

補充 yours 你（們）的東西
Please turn off your cell phone during a movie.
看電影期間，請將手機關機。

youth
[juθ]
名 青少年；青少年時期

The actress was a famous beauty in her youth.
這位女演員年輕時是出名的美人。

yummy
[`jʌmɪ]
形 好吃的

That Turkish restaurant has yummy ice cream.
那家土耳其餐廳供應的冰淇淋很美味。

Unit 25　Zz 字頭單字

MP3 25

zebra
[`zibrə]
名 斑馬

補充 giraffe 長頸鹿
Annie drew several giraffes and zebras on the paper.
安妮在紙上畫了幾隻長頸鹿和斑馬。

zero
[`zɪro]
形 零的 名 零

補充 centigrade 攝氏溫度的
In the winter, the temperature here is sometimes zero degrees centigrade.
這裡冬天的溫度有時會到攝氏零度。

zoo
[zu]
名 動物園

Many visitors come to the zoo to see the lovely pandas.
許多參觀者來動物園看可愛的熊貓。

NOTE

NOTE

NOTE

NOTE

國家圖書館出版品預行編目資料

強效衝刺!國中會考搶分英單2000／張翔 著. --初版. --
新北市:知識工場出版 采舍國際有限公司發行, 2023.1
面;公分 · --（試在必得 ; 02）
ISBN 978-986-271-945-9（平裝）

1.CST: 英語教學　2.CST: 詞彙　3.CST: 中等教育

524.38   111012616

知識工場・試在必得02

強效衝刺! 國中會考搶分英單2000

出 版 者／全球華文聯合出版平台・知識工場
作　　者／張翔
出版總監／王寶玲　　　　　　　　文字編輯／何牧蓉
總 編 輯／歐綾纖　　　　　　　　美術設計／May

台灣出版中心／新北市中和區中山路2段366巷10號10樓
電　　話／（02）2248-7896
傳　　真／（02）2248-7758
ISBN-13／978-986-271-945-9
出版日期／2023年

全球華文市場總代理／采舍國際
地　　址／新北市中和區中山路2段366巷10號3樓
電　　話／（02）8245-8786
傳　　真／（02）8245-8718

港澳地區總經銷／和平圖書
地　　址／香港柴灣嘉業街12號百樂門大廈17樓
電　　話／（852）2804-6687
傳　　真／（852）2804-6409

全系列書系特約展示
新絲路網路書店
地　　址／新北市中和區中山路2段366巷10號10樓
電　　話／（02）8245-9896
傳　　真／（02）8245-8819
網　　址／www.silkbook.com